# SOCIALISM vs CAPITALISM

## *Roosevelt to Obama*

*The Struggle to Achieve Balance in Government*

**SOCIALISM vs CAPITALISM**
*Roosevelt to Obama*

Copyright © 2013 by George Melvin Barney

All rights reserved. No part of this book may be used or reproduced by any means, graphic, electronic, or mechanical, including photocopying, recording, taping or by any information storage retrieval system without the written permission of the author or Merit Books except in the case of brief quotations embodied in critical articles and reviews.

*SOCIALISM vs CAPITALISM*
may be ordered by contacting:
Merit Books
3548 Golfing Green Drive
Farmers Branch, Texas  75234
www.mel-barney.com
e-mail: barney.mel@gmail.com


ISBN:  1493751344
Library of Congress Control Number  2013921631

First Edition
Printed in the United States of America

Cover Design by Jeanne Ann Macejko

# SOCIALISM
## vs
# CAPITALISM
## *Roosevelt to Obama*

*The Struggle to Achieve Balance in Government*

## Mel Barney

**Merit Books**

Dedicated to my wife Carolyn,
for her unwavering support during my writing of this book.

# CONTENTS

# 1% Earn 19.3% of U.S. Income

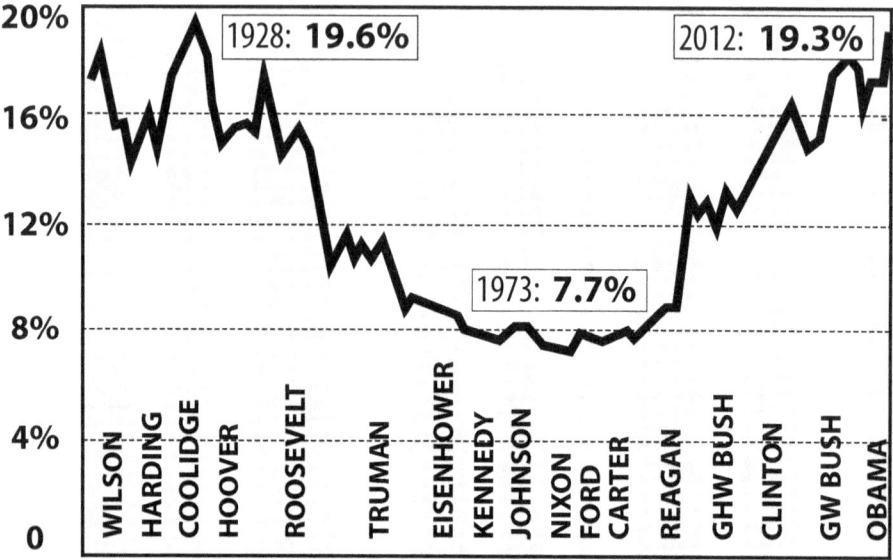

**Percentage of total U.S. income by top 1% of earners**

1928: **19.6%**

2012: **19.3%**

1973: **7.7%**

WILSON, HARDING, COOLIDGE, HOOVER, ROOSEVELT, TRUMAN, EISENHOWER, KENNEDY, JOHNSON, NIXON, FORD, CARTER, REAGAN, GHW BUSH, CLINTON, GW BUSH, OBAMA

SOURCE: World Top Incomes Database          The Associated Press to *Dallas Morning News*  9/11/13
(Facundo Alvaredo, Anthony B. Atkinson, Thomas Piketty, & Emmanuel Saez)
http://topincomesg-mond.parisschoolofeconomics.eu/09/11/2013

*Prior to the Great Depression, almost 20% of the national income was concentrated in the hands of the wealthiest 1%. After WWII, the middle class grew and prospered and our economy expanded. Since the Reagan era, the top 1% have amassed great wealth at the expense of the middle class and our once robust economy has faltered.*

# INTRODUCTION

**This book** covers the administrations of 13 U.S. Presidents who held that office during my lifetime. Each chapter discusses a President and the most important governmental activities and policy changes during his administration. These changes moved the country in a more socialistic or a more capitalistic direction. Each chapter defines the world situation, the economic health of the United States, and the political climate throughout the world.

Each chapter begins with a graphic which indicates the point along the socialism/capitalism continuum that characterizes that presidential administration.

▼

| SOCIALISM | CAPITALISM |
|---|---|

Most governments continually deal with this political balancing act between these two governing systems. There is a continuing contest between the well-organized wealthiest citizens to move the governing policies in the direction that would further enhance their wealthier status. The middle class and poor far outnumber those in the wealthier class, and these groups continually try to have implemented initiatives that would provide them with more opportunities for themselves and their children. This contest is an ongoing contest in all nations and particularly in the United States. These policies include better education, better national infrastructure, and a level playing field in terms of political competition with the very wealthy organizations. The wealthy organizations objectives are to privatize the many national functions such as education, highway construction, and infrastructure so that they may make a profit from these projects.

The chart on page *ii* (source: Worlds Top Income Database), shows the "Percentage of Total U. S. Income by Top 1% of Earners." An article in the *Dallas Morning News* on September 11, 2013, discussed this issue. The article compares the income of the richest 1% earners in the United States from 1920 through 2013. Note that during the early part of the Great Depression and today the highest earners had incomes of more than 19% of the total earned income in the United States.

Our nation became the unquestioned strongest economic and military nation in the world between the administrations of Roosevelt and Carter (1932-1980). The highest 1% income earner's portion of earned income was gradually reduced to less than 8% of the total income in the country, until the Reagan administration (1981-1989). From the Reagan Administration through the Obama Administration (1981-2013), the income of the wealthiest 1% increased to almost 20% of the total income of all of the United States.

After the start of 'Reaganomics,' the United States began losing the unquestioned world leadership, both economically and militarily. The Reagan Administration initiated the commencement of the Capitalism Period that we face today. It is frightening to highlight the similarities of the situation between the Great Depression and the problems our country faces today.

Many 'smoke screen issues' are used as propaganda tools to try to move the country in one direction or the other. These issues include religion, abortion, immigration, gun control, health care, unnecessary wars and military initiatives. These issues are used to systematically divert the citizens' attention from the initiatives that would benefit all of the nation's citizens.

During my 85 years, I have observed and participated in the forces that move nations between competing systems of socialism and capitalism. I have always had a strong interest in politics and governmental activities. I spent the last four years collecting specific information relating to this subject.

I had a freshman high school civics teacher who required that we read the editorial page each day. This became a habit for me since that time.

In my last book, FOUR WARS, I concentrated on the four wars that made major changes to the governing policies of the United States. These wars included the Great Depression, World War II, the Cold War, and the present global economic crisis.

Policies that lean toward oppressive Socialism or greedy Capitalism are established by the president and the members of congress who have been elected to these very important offices.

The changes in policies reflect the changes in the citizenry of the country during a particular president's lifetime. Today's electorate includes: those born before the great depression; the depression generation; the post-WWII baby boomer generation, the X and Y generations; and the Millennials. It is clear when studying the information presented that lessons learned prior to the Boomer generation were not passed satisfactorily to succeeding generations. Beginning in 1980, political power gradually diminished for those born prior to World War II. The great leaders of the 1930s through the 1970s were elected on the basis of what we had experienced during hard times. These leaders understood the policies required to direct the country to become the strongest economic and military power in the world.

After 1980, the younger generations gained political power and elected leaders who adopted dangerous policies that are driving our nation toward another Great Depression.

Policies initiated in the 1980s are causing the United States to lose its world economic and military dominance. Public reaction to these policies will ultimately drive our country in the direction of socialism. Current policies have created conditions that include: poverty; an uninformed, under-educated citizenry; and insufficient governmental transparency. When such conditions exist for a prolonged period of time, citizens will demand redress and drastic governmental changes will be the result.

The most damaging policies that result in capitalism incorporate a devious use of financial resources for the benefit of very wealthy citizens. The United

States, as well as other democratic nations, is strongest both economically and militarily when a large percentage of the population is economically defined as middle class.

I have categorized the presidential administrations of Roosevelt through Jimmy Carter as the *Shared Sacrifice Period (SSP)*. Those of us who experienced the Great Depression are heavily influenced by the policies carried out by those elected officials who were responsible for our economic and military guidance until 1980.

Ronald Reagan's terms (Reaganomics) through 2013, I refer to as the *Greed Initiative Period (GIP)*. During the *GIP*, influence of the depression generation diminished and was replaced by influences from the period of post-war prosperity including the 'Baby Boomer' and following generations.

Our *Shared Sacrifice Period (SSP)*, generation did many things right. However, we failed to teach the boomer generation the importance of thrift, shared responsibility, national infrastructure investment, as well as the dangers of the *Military Industrial Complex (MIC)*. President Eisenhower, who was one of our greatest generals, warned about the Military Industrial Complex in his farewell address as President.

The *SSP* generation realized that saving one penny of after-tax money was the equivalent of saving two pennies when you consider the requirements (education, transportation, etc.) for earning that penny in the first place. We realized that a strong public education system would provide a citizenry that was capable of competing in the modern technological world. Well-compensated public school teachers and well-equipped schools are the key to an educated, productive citizenry. (You get what you pay for.)

It is very important for the public to understand that educating a large number of students in math and science is required if we are to be the strongest economic and military power in the world.

Scientists and engineers are 'self proliferating.' The more they create and invent, the more there is to create and invent. Ultimately, the country with the strongest technology base will win both the military and economic world competition.

After World War II, many returning soldiers pursued advanced education and training to become scientists and engineers. The products they invented propelled the country into unquestioned world technology leadership for more than 45 years. Credit for this technology bonanza may be traced to good public schools, the G.I. Bill of Rights, and the Marshall plan.

Those wealthier and more influential citizens who dominate the Greed Initiatives Period (*GIP*) are continually fighting to reduce funding for public education. Because property taxes provide the funding for public education, it is in their personal financial interest to reduce or eliminate these taxes. Many of the wealthier citizens hire lawyers to make sure they pay unrealistically small property taxes. Their wealth allows them to enroll their children in private schools that generally have better educators than the public schools. Today America is not ranked in the top two dozen countries in the world in terms of public education. The short-term reduction in tax rates has resulted in the long-term decline in the skill level of the country's workforce. More funding and effort must be expended to increase the number of students who are proficient in math and science if our nation is to succeed in the economically competitive environment that exists today.

Between 1980 and today, the average corporate tax went from approximately 40% to approximately 30%. The average infrastructure spending went from approximately 5% to 1%. Infrastructure investments include rail, telecommunications, electrical power generation, water resources, etc. In addition to the increasing national debt, these changes have resulted in neglected highway maintenance and other essential national infrastructure investments.

The wealthy and powerful prefer a volunteer military over a military draft system. Without the draft, our military forces are largely comprised of the sons and daughters of those with limited economic and educational options. Those families with greater financial means have far less incentive to enter the military services. With a military draft system, powerful influencers would be less likely to start a military confrontation that might place their own children at risk. Wealthy corporations and industries have a vested interest in promoting military production and foreign wars. Their investments in the Military Industrial Complex increase in value whenever the country has a dispute or war with another nation. The profitability in the manufacture and sale of weapons of war favors military action over diplomacy and drives the intensity of confrontations with other nations.

The relative cost in terms of fuel to transport freight or people over railways as opposed to highways is about 15%. This means that using railroads as our primary transportation provider would cost about 1/7 the amount of fuel it would take to transport the equivalent load over our highway system. One has to experience the comfort and convenience that most advanced nation's railway systems have provided for their citizens to appreciate this fact. These countries pay for these wonderful railway systems with high fuel taxes on their highway trucks and automobiles.

Oil and coal companies, construction companies, automobile companies, and financial institutions influence our politicians to build more roadways rather than more efficient railways. Toll roads also contribute wealth to those who invest in these monstrous, pollution-generating, maintenance-devouring expenses. Toll road expenses take a much higher percentage of family income from the low income groups than the high income groups.

Investments in national infrastructure make the country more valuable. This is proven by initiatives like the Tennessee Valley Authority, the Transcontinental Railroad, the Panama Canal, the Interstate Highway System, the National Park System, and dozens of other initiatives that have resulted in large dividends, decade after decade. The nation has enjoyed many times the original investments in these national initiatives.

In my evaluation of the 13 presidents, I have chosen not to discuss behavioral mistakes. I concentrate on those presidential initiatives that balance the governmental policies between the very wealthy and the struggling poor and middle class citizens within the country. A nation is strongest when a strong well informed citizenry pays close attention to what their politicians are doing.

This introduction has presented my opinions about the politics, economics and military pursuits of the country. My background may explain the reasons I have espoused these opinions.

One may also choose to explore my credentials and attitude toward important issues by examining Chapter XIV. I have included some of my published letters to the editor of the *Dallas Morning News*.

My credentials for writing **SOCIALISM VERSUS CAPITALISM** are well chronicled in my book **FOUR WARS**. I earned my Masters Degree in Electrical Engineering at SMU. My engineering career was devoted to inventing and selling classified military weapons of war. I have been awarded six patents, mostly for classified military systems. I traveled and have done business in 54 different countries as an engineer with Texas Instruments. Many of these trips were in cooperation with and sometimes encouraged by the CIA. My adventurous life included spy trips to Russia in cooperation with the CIA during the Cold War, and a period as the Manager of TI activities in Washington, DC.

# I.

# ROOSEVELT

## (1933-1945)

## *World Hero*

▼

SOCIALISM   CAPITALISM

The United States was fortunate to have elected a brilliant leader like Franklin Delano Roosevelt as President in 1932. He understood the drastic circumstances the country faced both in the depression and World War II.

He implemented major changes in our government policies that were sometimes dictatorial.

He was the only president ever elected to four presidential terms. This proves that the people trusted his leadership. He assumed dictatorial powers to save our nation. His tenure in office places him in a more Socialism status than any other president during my lifetime. He was required by the situation, including the Great Depression and World War II, to assume a more **socialistic rating.**

# The Great Depression

When Roosevelt took office on March 4, 1933 the United States was deep in the depression that was started by the Wall Street collapse in 1929. Significant actions had to be taken to restore a reasonable economic foundation for the country. Roosevelt did some brilliant planning to solve the problems that the country was experiencing. He had strong political opposition. He took actions that improved the economic situation for all of the American citizens.

In the next seven years, his actions were both effective and comforting for most U.S. citizens. Many of the actions he took were opposed by more conservative citizens. They felt that he was moving the government too far in the direction of socialism. The citizens were correct in their assessment. Roosevelt's actions were in fact necessary to steer the country toward economic stability.

When he took office approximately 1% of the population was receiving almost 20% of the income generated by the entire U.S. economic system. This situation created real problems for the middle class to maintain a reasonable standard of living and to properly educate their children.

Many of us who lived through the depression, remember Roosevelt's 'fireside chats.' He communicated directly with all of the people by radio. Families would sit in front of their radio sets and listen to Roosevelt's state of the nation speeches. These fireside chats were instrumental in rebuilding confidence in our government's ability to correct the nation's economic problems. One of his most famous comments was, "We have nothing to fear but fear itself." Franklin Roosevelt was a genius at public relations.

His public relations prowess was so strong that he changed a very stubborn Congress to one that supported the activities and initiatives that he felt were necessary to restore the United States to its strong economic position in the world.

His goal in the first 100 days was to enact programs that would immediately affect the economic well-being of all of the citizens. Some of his initiatives included: closing of the banks (which the citizens no longer trusted); the enactment of the Federal Deposit Insurance Corporation (FDIC) (which provided government insurance to protect the depositors accounts up to some level of their deposits); passing the Agricultural Adjustment Administration Act (which saved many farmers from bankruptcy); and the Civilian Conservation Corps (which provided a job for any able person who wanted to work).

The Glass-Stegall Act was part of the banking bill that insured the depositor's savings accounts up to a specific limit. It also prevented the bank executives from gambling with the depositor's money on the stock market. This act was later repealed under the heavy influence of Phil Gramm during the Bill Clinton administration. As will be discussed later, this action was largely responsible for creating the financial crises in 1998 and 2008.

These initiatives were all socialistic. Many citizens accused Roosevelt of being a socialist and a dictator. These same feelings exist in some politicians to this date. Call it what you may but, Roosevelt was able to restore a reasonable economic process.

Other programs were added to Roosevelt's 'NEW DEAL' in 1935. One was the Works Projects Administration (WPA). The WPA offered employment for artists, writers, musicians, and authors. Another program was the Social Security Act which provided unemployment compensation and protection against poverty when the citizens reached advanced ages.

The citizens of the United States had developed such a confidence in Roosevelt that they elected him four times. All of his elections in 1936, 1940, and 1944 were won by sizable voter margins.

After the 1936 election, significant opposition to the NEW DEAL initiatives developed. The legality of some of his programs was challenged at the Supreme Court level. He tried to add two members to the Supreme Court, in an effort to defeat these challenges. He failed, but most of his NEW DEAL initiatives remained intact.

In June of 1938, Congress passed his minimum wage act, which required that employers pay their workers a minimum of $.25 an hour. Within a few years, this was raised to $.40 an hour.

In April of 1939, Hitler occupied Czechoslovakia. This was followed by the invasion of Poland. World War II was now underway and Hitler's next targets included the Netherlands and France.

In 1939, Prime Minister Winston Churchill of Britain and President Roosevelt started meeting to discuss the world war that was developing between the Axis Powers (Germany, Italy, Japan) and the Allies ( Great

Britain, France, Russia, and the United States). Both leaders were extraordinarily intelligent and became great friends. Their plans to win the war included a pledge that there would be no peace agreement signed until all Axis powers had agreed to **unconditional surrender.**

The United States declared that it would be the **"Arsenal of democracy"** for the Allied Forces. By1939, the United States was sending war supplies to Europe in large convoys across the Atlantic Ocean. German Navy U-boats began sinking our ships carrying supplies to our allies in Europe.

As the United States moved closer to a declaration of war, Roosevelt initiated one of the most secret weapons development programs the world has ever known—the atomic bomb. In October 1939, Dr. Albert Einstein advised President Roosevelt that the Germans were developing an atomic bomb, and that we should use all means to develop the atomic bomb before the Germans could complete their weapon. On October 21, 1939, Roosevelt set up a committee headed by Lyman Briggs who was the director of the Bureau of Standards. The objective of this committee was to outline a program to develop an atomic bomb before Hitler could do the same. This became known as the Manhattan project. The headquarters of this project was in Oak Ridge, Tennessee.

The investment in the atomic bomb was so massive it is hard to imagine. Keeping the program secret during World War II was an absolute miracle. Even Vice President Harry Truman was not aware that this weapon was being developed until after President Roosevelt died.

Dr. Robert Oppenheimer was the Director of this program. His laboratory was located beneath the football stadium at the University of Chicago. The final product was produced at a secret facility in Oak Ridge, Tennessee. Thousands of people were employed at this facility. Only a few of those who worked on the atomic bomb knew what they were working on.

A third facility was set up in Los Alamos, New Mexico. The purpose of this facility was to test the final explosive capabilities of this new weapon of mass destruction. A precise measuring instrumentation network was constructed to determine the level of destruction the atomic bomb would produce. Prior to the first test explosion at Las Alamos, no one was sure just how destructive the atomic bomb would be. All of this effort paid off by allowing the United States to end the war with Japan without invading Japan.

On June 10, 1940, France surrendered to Hitler. President Roosevelt went before Congress and asked for 1.3 billion dollars to build up the armed forces. He told the nation that our country would align itself with the Western European countries against the Axis powers.

During 1940, the British were being bombarded from both the air and sea by the Germans. On September 3, 1940, the United States provided old warships to the British for their battle against Hitler.

On September 12, 1940, the United States put a ban on all oil and scrap metal shipments to the Japanese. This action infuriated the military establishment in Japan.

On November 5, 1940, Roosevelt won a sweeping

victory over Wendell Willkie and became the first president in U.S. history to be elected to more than two terms in office. The population at that time was 131,000,000.

# World War II

With the war clouds thickening in Europe, Roosevelt's influence with the public helped defeat the very strong antiwar opposition of many influential congressional leaders.

From September of 1939 when Germany invaded Poland until the official war between the United States against Japan, Germany, and Italy began in December of 1941, an amazing transformation of the United States took place. There were plenty of jobs for everyone and everyone had money to spend. The problem was that we could not produce enough goods to fill the military and civilian needs. Rationing of almost everything was started. Taxes were raised and a war tax was added.

The highest income tax bracket during Roosevelt's term of office was 70%. He also included a new excess profits tax on those entrepreneurs who were making millions of dollars manufacturing military supplies. In addition to these taxing strategies, publicity promoted the purchase of war bonds. Roosevelt's objective was to pay the cost of World War II as we progressed in our war effort. Here again, an element of the electorate felt he was moving far too rapidly toward a socialistic form of government. Roosevelt, on the other hand, knew that he had to impose big policy changes on the country in order to win the war. It is certainly notable and should be studied by those generations following Roosevelt's terms that *World War II was won in a matter of 45 months*. Compare this with the length of time we have spent on all subsequent wars, many of which have been unsuccessful.

Roosevelt's greatest public relations talents were to keep the public aware of the situation and remind them that a **shared sacrifice attitude** would be required to win the war.

Thousands of posters reminded the public of the critical importance of the war. "Loose lips sink ships," a picture of Uncle Sam saying "I want you," and "Buy War Bonds."

On October 29, 1941, the drafting of men who were 21 to 36 years old commenced. Henry Stemson, Secretary of War, drew the first number. It was 158. This meant that the men born on June 8, the 158th day of the year, would be the first ones called in the military draft. One by one, Congressmen selected the remaining numbers. These numbers represented the sequence of birthdays of the individuals being drafted into military service. It was not long before all able bodied men were being drafted.

At one time during the war, there were 10 million Americans in military service. There were some women serving in each branch of the military services. Women in the U.S. Army Air Corps ferried warplanes to combat areas, leaving men to operate these aircraft on combat missions. Many women were also performing civilian jobs previously done by men. Tens of thousands of women worked in war plants building airplanes, tanks and other weapons. All of these activities gave the population of the country a different perspective on the idea that 'a woman's place was in the home.' Ultimately, this gave women greater equality.

Roosevelt set up some amazing war material production facilities. Three one-mile-long aircraft manufacturing buildings were built. They turned out warplanes as fast as one aircraft a day. These buildings were leased to the aircraft manufacturers and are still being used to build military aircraft for the armed services today. One is located in Tulsa, Oklahoma, one in Fort Worth, Texas, and the third is located in Marietta, Georgia. Roosevelt knew this kind of big policy thinking was necessary for the country to win World War II. Local politics in the areas where these factories were located have kept these factories open and operating ever since World War II. In many cases, they are now building unneeded war machines. Some of the equipment currently being built in these factories has been obsolete for as long as two wars ago.

Roosevelt also constructed shipbuilding facilities that were turning out one ship a day. Unfortunately for our country, these factories were not converted to civilian use to build infrastructure such as railroad and communications equipment.

Every U.S. citizen was involved in the war effort, even the children. Drives collected scrap metal, tinfoil, rubber, and any other materials that could be used in war production. While in the seventh grade, I sold war stamps. These stamps were placed in books to buy war bonds. When $7.50 worth of stamps was pasted in the book, the book could be traded for a war bond that would be worth $10 after 10 years. Once a week, teachers would read *My Weekly Reader*. This publication reported what happened to our military forces in the past week. The articles were written in language that grammar school students could easily understand. Sometimes the Allied Forces would have won significant victories and sometimes they experienced defeats. These communications kept every man, woman, and child, educated and involved in our 'do or die' situation during World War II.

One of the primary differences between World War II and the wars that we have fought since that time is that all of the citizens of the country were involved and affected by the war effort. Most of this attitude should be attributed to Roosevelt's understanding of what it took to win the war.

Many immigrants from and descendants of families of the Axis Nations (Germany, Italy, and Japan), lived and worked within the United States. Some were known sympathizers who supplied sensitive strategic military information to the Axis Powers. These sympathizers were labeled the 'the Fifth Column.' This term had been used first by Ernest Hemingway in his play about the 1936 Spanish Civil War.

Roosevelt and his advisors worked diligently to identify and prosecute Axis sympathizers and spies within the United States. One kind of sabotage fifth columnists provided was the timing of war material shipments to Europe. This information gave German submarines the locations and timing of cargo ships carrying military supplies to our Allies.

On December 7, 1941, the Japanese made a surprise

attack on the United States at Pearl Harbor, Hawaii. This attack caught U.S. military establishment and government by complete surprise. The excuse given by the military for this surprise attack was that they were expecting a flight of B-17 bombers from the United States. When the Japanese warplanes first showed up on the radar scopes of the Hawaiian defensive radar systems, the U.S. military leaders assumed it was the flight of B-17s scheduled to arrive from the United States. Most of the battleships of the U.S. Pacific Fleet were lined up along Battleship Row in the Hawaiian Harbor. Most were so damaged that they were practically useless. It took many months for the few battleships that could be repaired to be returned to fight the Pacific war. Fortunately, all of the aircraft carriers in the Pacific Fleet were out at sea and were undamaged by the attack. As the Pacific war progressed over the next two years, the aircraft carrier turned out to be far more effective than the large battleships that were put out of commission at Pearl Harbor.

Within days after the Japanese attacked Pearl Harbor, both Germany and Italy declared war on the United States. Roosevelt enlisted the help of Hollywood to support his initiatives by using the most famous movie stars such as Shirley Temple (to produce 'happy' movies) and encouraged Hollywood to produce movies that would educate the public and raise the spirits of the country. Many of the Hollywood stars supported Roosevelt's activities in promoting the United Service Organization (USO). He sent world famous movie stars to entertain our soldiers both at home and overseas. He encouraged well known stars such as Bob Hope and Bing Crosby to participate in USO tours around the world to entertain our troops in the field. He asked George M. Cohan to write patriotic songs. He also recognized those with family members serving in the war. There were dozens of other initiatives pursued by Roosevelt's administration. They were intended to divert the attention of the nation from the desperate military and economic conditions that existed in the country during the World War II period.

One action taken by the Roosevelt administration was highly criticized to this day. On February 19, 1942, 110,000 Japanese-Americans, most of whom lived on the West Coast, were relocated to camps in the country's interior and their personal property impounded.

On February 23, 1942, a Japanese submarine shelled the Richfield oil refinery at Santa Barbara, California. The attack did minimum damage. It did create an atmosphere of anxiety. Americans began to fear an attack on the U.S. mainland by the Japanese military forces.

On April 18, 1942, Col. James Doolittle attacked Tokyo from an aircraft carrier in the Pacific Ocean. This was accomplished with a squadron of the B-25 Bombers flying from an aircraft carrier. Although the damage to Tokyo was not devastating, it did two things for the country. One was to raise the morale of the American public, so that they would understand that we were going to aggressively attack Japan. It also sent a message to the Japanese that their country was vulnerable to attack from our military forces.

During the 1942 period, the Russians were losing the war on the Eastern front in Europe and Great

Britain and the United States were losing the war in Western Europe and in the Pacific area. The invasion of France by Germany had been successful and Germany was in control of France.

Roosevelt was not only deeply involved in the strategic planning of the military initiatives of World War II, he also had to deal with the American public. On December 27, 1943, the railroad workers threatened to strike. Roosevelt warned both the union and the management that the government would take over the railroads if they did not settle their differences. The strike was averted.

In late November 1943, the three Allied leaders (Stalin, Churchill, and Roosevelt) met in Tehran, Iran. They made some important decisions and came to agreements on four very basic strategic plans. One was that they would all continue the war until all of the Axis Powers were defeated. The second agreement was that the Allies would start an invasion of Western Europe in order to relieve the Russians who were losing the battle in Eastern Europe. The third agreement was that once the Axis Powers in Europe were defeated, Russia would then turn its war machine against the Japanese. The fourth agreement was that once the Axis Powers in Europe had been conquered, the Allies would sit down and agree which geographic areas would be under the control of Russia, Great Britain, the United States, and France.

Roosevelt was vigorously criticized by political conservatives in the United States, because he reached agreement with the Russians who were espousing communism over capitalism in the sectors that were under Russian Control. Under the circumstances that prevailed, it was a tough call for Roosevelt.

One of the most difficult decisions Roosevelt had to make was to put tens of thousands of U.S. lives on the line in order to invade Europe. It was with great trepidation that he and General Eisenhower agreed upon the invasion in early June of 1944. Roosevelt agreed on a plan put together by Eisenhower and the leaders of France and Great Britain to invade Europe in the Normandy area of France. From the many books that have been written about this invasion, it has to have been the worst military experience ever endured by both the Allied and Axis powers.

The next meeting of Roosevelt, Churchill and Stalin was in Yalta in early February 1945. It was becoming obvious that the Allied Nations would soon be able to declare victory over the Axis Powers. At this meeting the three leaders divided the European countries that would be retaken from the Germans. There would be a Russian, British, French, and United States boundary agreement over the re-conquered territory. Roosevelt again received much criticism from the most conservative U.S. citizenry.

Most of the actions taken by Roosevelt both during the Great Depression and World War II leaned heavily toward socialism. However, in order to win the war, these were necessary initiatives.

Unfortunately, President Roosevelt passed away on April 12, 1945. He did not experience the satisfaction of defeating the Axis Powers. President Roosevelt left the country with policies that changed the culture of the country. Many of his NEW DEAL policies are still in effect. His policies provided a more balanced democracy for all U.S. citizens. Most citizens who lived through the period of the Great Depression and World War II have benefitted from the policies of his administration.

Since Roosevelt had passed away and Churchill had been defeated by Clement Atlee in Great Britain, neither of these great leaders attended the next Allied Conference in Potsdam, Germany. This conference included Clement Atlee, Harry Truman, and Joseph Stalin. The seeds of the Cold War were planted at this conference that officially divided the territories of Europe that had been reclaimed from the Axis Powers.

Franklin Roosevelt was probably the one president who came closest to being a dictator in U.S. history. He took strong, decisive positions in order to beat the depression and win this most difficult of all wars.

**Mel Barney**

# II.

# TRUMAN

## (1945-1953)

## *Policies Produced*
## *World's Greatest Superpower*

▼

| SOCIALISM | CAPITALISM |

**Harry Truman**, who served in World War I, was the type of leader that we needed after World War II. He knew that in order to have a strong United States, we also had to help reconstruct the damage done by this very destructive war. His Marshall plan and the insistence on a strong GI Bill of Rights established the United States as the most advanced technological country in the world.

He was a no-nonsense person and was willing to take criticism from his many political opponents. He worked with them to solve the problems facing the country. His main objective was to prove capitalism was far better than socialism. He deserves a rating of a **balanced democracy.**

When Truman took office, he retained all of the Roosevelt cabinet. He requested that they feel free to advise him of their thoughts about what actions Roosevelt would have taken under the new circumstances.

He was the only president over the last 100 years who did not have a college education. However, most of the citizenry trusted Truman's common sense, honesty, and feeling of duty toward our country's destiny.

The war in Europe ended when the German leaders led by Grand Admiral Karl Doenitz signed an 'unconditional surrender document' on May 7, 1945. President Roosevelt's death on April 12, 1945, left Truman to deal with the problem of conquering a very determined Japanese nation. He had been promised support by the Russians in defeating the Japanese. Truman faced another huge invasion of Japan that would cost the lives of tens of thousands of U.S. soldiers and sailors and uncounted Japanese citizens and Japanese armed forces. An invasion of Japan would also cost billions of dollars.

The Potsdam Conference in July of 1945 included Clement Attlee, Stalin, and Truman. During this meeting, Truman advised Stalin that the United States had developed the atomic bomb. Stalin's spy network had already advised Stalin that this was the case. At this meeting, Truman received word that the atomic bomb tests at Los Alamos had been successful.

In his arsenal, Truman now had the atomic bomb. To this day, there are those who argue that Truman should not have used this weapon of mass destruction on the civilians of Nagasaki and Hiroshima. Those soldiers and sailors who were involved in the Pacific war are almost 100% supportive of Truman's actions in the use of the bombs. Within days of deployment, the Japanese Empire was forced to surrender unconditionally.

On August 6, 1945, the first atomic bomb was dropped on the city of Hiroshima and was quickly followed two days later with an atomic bomb dropped on the city of Nagasaki. A total of approximately 130,000 Japanese citizens were killed by these two military operations.

On September 2, 1945, General MacArthur signed the Japanese unconditional surrender document. The ceremony took place on the battleship Missouri in Tokyo Harbor.

Truman substantially moved the U.S. policies in a more capitalistic direction. He offset many of the dictatorial and socialistic initiatives that had been required to reverse the depression and win World War II. Many Roosevelt 'New Deal' initiatives remained. Harry Truman brought back the incentives in his 'Fair Deal' Programs to promote a strong capitalistic system. With the end of the depression and World War II, Truman was able to move our country in a more moderate direction.

On August 17, 1945, Russia and the United States divided Korea along the 38th parallel. The Russians immediately set up barriers to prevent any exchange between the two new nations.

In August 1945, Truman introduced his new 'Fair Deal.' He recommended to Congress a 21-point program to return the country to a peacetime economy. He ordered the resumption of production of consumer products, free markets, and collective bargaining. His message included his comment that "Every segment of the population and, every individual had a right to expect from his government a Fair Deal." All rationing ended by December 31, 1945. An important part of Truman's programs included lifting of price controls. The GI Bill of Rights commenced the education of many returning servicemen and jobs were provided for returning servicemen.

In the early part of 1946, many of the country's largest companies went on strike. Truman had already received no-strike pledges from the large union bosses by convincing them that negotiations were the best way to prevent these strikes. In April of 1946, the United Mine Workers went on strike. Truman ordered the government to take over the operation of the mines and John L. Lewis, the leader of the UMW, was fined $10,000. The union was fined $3,500,000. This action sent a message to the union leaders that negotiations were the best procedure for settling labor/management disputes.

On March 5, 1946, Winston Churchill, who had already been replaced by Clement Attlee, commented "An iron curtain has descended across the continent." This comment served notice to the world that the Cold War between communism and democracy had commenced. The European continent was split between the eastern portion which was controlled by the Soviet Union and the western portion which was controlled by the Allied Nations.

Truman faced other extremely difficult issues. One of the worst problems was finding jobs for the millions of military personnel who were returning to civilian life. Many jobs that had been promised to these military veterans no longer existed. One of the brighter aspects of this situation was that soldiers who could not find jobs had access through the GI Bill of Rights to a college education. A total of four million returning military service personnel were educated on the GI Bill of Rights.

The wartime price controls that had been placed on commodities had to be lifted and inflation became a significant problem. In fact, the inflation rate skyrocketed 6% in one month alone.

Dozens of wartime changes had to be made during peace time by Truman and his administration. One of the worst situations was a massive strike of the steel unions that sent 800,000 workers onto the picket line. At the same time, coal miners and railroad workers went on strike. Then farmers refused to sell their products at prices which had been frozen during the war.

The United States and our Allies were causing many problems for the Russians, particularly in Berlin. Under the Russians and the Allies, Berlin had been divided into separate sectors. The Allied sectors of Berlin were outperforming the Russian sections economically to the extent that Germans in the Russian sector were desperately trying to get into Allied-controlled sectors. It became so embarrassing, that on July 24, 1948, the Soviet Union blocked all ground access to the three Western Allied sectors of Berlin. Even basic supplies could not be delivered to the German citizens in those areas.

Instead of using military force, Truman initiated what is now known as the Berlin Airlift. The Berlin

Airlift provided all of the needed supplies to the Allied sectors of Berlin by using transport aircraft that delivered their cargoes to Berlin's Templehof Airbase. This turned out to be a great victory for Truman. On May 11, 1949, the Russians relented and opened up the ground transportation systems.

The Berlin situation caused the Cold War to heat up. The Cold War threatened nuclear chaos for both the communist and democratic nations. All U.S. presidents starting with Truman and concluding with Nixon maintained the Cold War as one of their highest priorities. The Russians and United States spent billions of dollars building weapons and counter weapons for the Cold War. It was only after the Nixon administration that the Cold War began to 'cool down.' As the reader will see, in the Nixon Chapter, Richard Nixon was largely responsible for ending the Cold War. The United States won this conflict by producing superior high-technology weapons.

In early 1947, many people in the country were leaning toward communistic policies. In order to counter this movement, Truman asked for and received $400 million to fight communism in Greece and Turkey as well as some elements in the United States. He also ordered loyalty checks for all government employees.

Earlier in February 17, 1947, Truman had initiated 'Voice of America' broadcasts in the Russian language. Radio beams were directed into Russia from radio stations located in countries that were friendly to the United States.

In 1947, the U.S. Congress passed the Taft-Hartley

Act. This act put new restrictions on unions and the formation of unions that made it very difficult for unions to organize, negotiate and to take decisive action to obtain higher wages and benefits. Truman vetoed the Taft-Hartley Act. Truman's veto was overridden by a U.S. Congress that was impatient with the numerous labor strikes and threatened strikes of union groups.

On June 23, 1947, the Taft-Hartley Act was passed over President Truman's veto. This act allowed the President to obtain an 80-day injunction against any strike and appoint a board of inquiry to oversee the collective bargaining. The act banned closed shops and gave the states more latitude in fighting organized labor drives. In retrospect, the passing of this act resulted in gains for the Democrats in the 1948 election.

On June 5, 1947, Truman's Secretary of State George C. Marshall announced his plan to rebuild the European countries, including both our allies and Axis enemies.

On November 25, 1947, the House of Representatives Un-American Activities Committee (HUAC) summoned many actors, directors and other Hollywood notables to testify before the committee. The objective of the HUAC was to identify and discourage any communist or communist sympathizers who were part of this Hollywood group. Notables among the many who testified included Gary Cooper, George Murphy and Ronald Reagan. Ronald Reagan at that time was the President of the Screen Actors Guild. Ten of those who testified or refused to testify before the committee were blacklisted by the industry.

Many of the soldiers who had fought in World War II remained in the reserve armed forces. Many were called back to duty when hostilities broke out later when North Korea attacked South Korea.

Due to the pressures from both Europe and eastern Asia, President Truman signed an order that reinstated the draft on June 24, 1948.

Truman, whose approval rating after the Japanese surrender had been 82% positive, was ultimately reduced to 32% as the 1948 elections approached.

On May 10, 1948, the railroad union went on strike. Truman forcibly ended the strike by having the government assume control of the nation's railroads. He declared that these labor disputes would be settled through mediation between the opposing groups.

With the 1948 elections coming up, many of Truman's initiatives received negative feedback from both Congress and American citizens. Senator Fulbright of Arkansas suggested that President Truman resign. Truman responded that he didn't care what Senator 'Halfbright' of Arkansas thought.

Within two weeks of the Democratic presidential nomination in 1948, Truman issued an executive order that racially integrated all of the armed services. This infuriated the southern block of Democrats who had fought against racial integration since the Civil War.

The 1948 presidential election featured a third-party identified as the Dixiecrats. It was led by then-governor of South Carolina Strom Thurman. This was a coalition of politicians who had fought to maintain racial segregation.

At that time, the three leading national polls were the Roper poll, the Crossley poll, and the Gallup poll. All three polls agreed that Truman would lose the 1948 presidential election by a high margin. Polling information was obtained through the use of telephones. What these polls did not take into consideration was the fact that many more Republican families were able to afford telephones than Democratic families. As a result, their polling numbers were erroneously skewed toward the Republican candidate. In 1948, Truman surprisingly won the election against Republican Thomas Dewey and Dixiecrat Strom Thurmond.

On November 3, 1948, Harry Truman was reelected President in one of the biggest presidential election upsets in U.S. history.

Truman was sworn in to his second term as President on January 20, 1949. For the first time television carried his inaugural address to 10 million television viewers as far west as Sedalia, Illinois. His policies were far more oriented toward cooperation with those nations who were striving for Democratic structures of government. He promised to help the poor nations by providing them with food, education, technology and equipment. He was a big supporter of continued cooperative activities with NATO.

The 'Truman Doctrine,' supported the United Nations and the setting aside of territory in Palestine for an Israeli Nation. On May 14, 1948, the United States recognized the state of Israel as an independent nation.

One of the most brilliant capitalistic initiatives ever undertaken was the Marshall Plan. Developed by Truman and General George C. Marshall, the plan cost our already deeply-indebted nation $13 billion. This plan enabled European countries, including the Axis nations, to rebuild their devastated cities, infrastructure and industrial base.

The United States reaped both admiration and extremely valuable economic leverage from the countries rebuilt under this plan. GI Bill of Rights, college-educated soldiers formed an elite, technologically-oriented workforce which created the world's most powerful national economic engine ever known. Four million GIs took advantage of the GI Bill of Rights by 1947.

The Marshall Plan provided the customer base for the new products that the educated veterans of the United States were inventing and producing. It is important to note that in 1940, 5% of the adult population in the United States had college degrees. By 1950, this number had jumped to 20%. As an engineer, I understand that the more an engineer or scientist invents, the more there is to invent and develop. A large number of the returning veterans, having been exposed to advanced technological weapons during the war, became engineers.

Unfortunately, the capitalist ideals of the United States were in direct opposition to the socialistic ideals of Russia. The Cold War began almost immediately after the Axis powers and Japan surrendered. The Russians could not offset the power and influence gained by the U.S. through the Marshall Plan and their college-educated veterans. This technological advantage lasted for over 40 years.

The attitude of *shared sacrifice* by all of the citizens of the country was gradually replaced with an attitude of capitalism. The average maximum tax rate during this 40-year period (1940 through 1980) was approximately 80% on higher income earners. Early in the Reagan administration, the 80% income tax rate for the highest-earning American citizens was drastically reduced. Since that time, the maximum tax rate on the highest-earning American citizens has been approximately 33%. This tax structure has produced considerably more financial pressure on the middle class and lower income citizens who carry an increasing larger burden for funding the federal government.

On June 25, 1950, North Korea invaded South Korea. It was a surprise attack and North Korea was close to annexing the whole of South Korea. Truman's first reaction was to use the U.S. Navy to blockade North Korea. However, funding for the U.S. Navy had been so drastically cut, the United States did not have the resources to execute this blockade.

Truman went to the United Nations and appealed for resources to force North Korea to remove their military forces from South Korea. He was successful in this endeavor and General Douglas MacArthur was given the responsibility to direct this military initiative.

General MacArthur planned a brilliant invasion action on the North Western coast of Korea at Inchon, which was not very far from the capital city of Seoul. This invasion drove the North Korean forces north to the Yalu River, the boundary between China and North Korea. China responded by sending a massive army to fight the United Nations troops. This action ended in a stalemate between the two opposing forces along the 38th parallel that divides North and South Korea.

MacArthur presented a plan to Truman to attack the Chinese supply lines west of the Yalu River. Truman did not want to start a new war with China and denied General MacArthur's plan. General MacArthur threatened to conduct the attack without Truman's approval. Truman immediately fired General MacArthur. Although both Congress and citizens of the United States reacted negatively at the dismissal of a World War II hero, Truman asserted the principle of civilian control of the military and avoided a long, bloody conflict with China.

The stalemate at the 38th parallel continued for two years during which 30,000 U.S. soldiers were killed. Finally, an armistice was agreed in 1953. Although this armistice stopped the shooting war, the animosity between North and South Korea continues 60 years later.

Truman had other troubles in the northern Pacific. The United States had been supporting General Chiang Kai-shek and his government against the communist leader Mao Zedong since 1930. In June 1950, Mao had driven General Chiang Kai-shek off mainland China and General Chiang Kai-shek had established the Republic of China on the island of Formosa off of the Chinese coast. Formosa is now referred to as Taiwan. In order for the United States to protect General Chiang Kai-shek from invasion by the communist dictator Mao Zedong, Truman ordered the U.S. Navy Seventh Fleet to the area so that Chiang Kai-shek's new Republic could not be occupied. With the passing of World War II and the new, yet unsolved Korean standoff, many Americans were becoming tired of fighting wars overseas. They were also very concerned about communist aggression throughout the globe. Then in 1949, the U.S. citizenry learned that Russia had exploded an atomic weapon.

On July 21, 1949, the Senate ratified the North Atlantic Treaty Organization. The main purpose of this organization was to unite member nations so that if any of the NATO Countries were attacked by other countries, NATO would come to their defense. A total of 12 countries were included in NATO.

On November 5, 1949, the Congress of Industrial Organizations threw out the unions that had communist affiliations.

Truman was not eligible to run for President in 1952 because Congress enacted the 22nd Amendment to the U.S. Constitution, which prevented a president from serving more than two terms in office. Included was a provision that presidents who served more than two years of a previous president's term were deemed to have served a full term.

Truman was well aware of the potential for the United States to move toward Communistic policies. Fortunately he was smart enough to guide the country away from these dangers.

Truman was fair to the unions, however, he did not let them disrupt the country's move toward a stable, capitalistic nation. The policies that he was able to establish provided the foundation for the United States to become the most powerful economic and military nation in the world and remain so for more than 40 years.

Truman's honesty and common sense were the result of being raised in a typical American community of Independence, Missouri. Truman had fought in World War I and had worked in a haberdashery shop before being elected to Congress. He was a very practical person who tried to establish a win-win situation wherever possible. One of his famous sayings was, "If you want a friend in Washington, get a dog."

Most of those of us who remember Harry Truman, think of him as a loyal U.S. citizen who was dedicated to doing the right thing for the United States. He appeared to be a politician that could not be 'bought.' He retired quietly with his wife Bess in his hometown of Independence, Missouri.

# III.
# EISENHOWER
## (1953-1961)

### *Championed Infrastructure: Opposed Military Spending*

**Dwight Eisenhower** was a military leader who knew the sting of sending military forces into battles where they could be killed or wounded. He hated war. He also knew that if you were going to have a strong country, you must have a strong, educated middle class to purchase the products built in the country. He was a farm boy who grew up during the depression in Kansas and truly had the best interest of the United States as his guiding principles. He was a very successful president and was responsible for building the Interstate Highway System.

Eisenhower deserves a rating slightly **Left of a Balanced Democracy.**

On November 5, 1952, General Dwight D. Eisenhower (Ike) defeated Adlai Stevenson and became the 34th President of the United States. Eisenhower ran on a platform that stressed winning the Korean War, eliminating the corruption within the government, and an all-out fight against communism.

Fulfilling one of his promises on December 5, 1952, Eisenhower went to Korea to visit our troops.

Ike took the oath of office on January 20, 1953. One of his first priorities was to bring peace to the war between North and South Korea. On July 27, 1953, a truce was signed between the United Nations and North Korea in Panmunjom. In addition to the more than 50,000 killed and 100,000 wounded, the war had been very costly.

In an action that was favored by Ike, the Supreme Court struck down the separate but equal status in the Brown versus Board of Education decision on May 17, 1954.

Eisenhower continued most of the 'New Deal,' GI Bill and Marshall Plan policies. He racially-integrated the government, and was responsible for the initiative to build the Interstate Highway System. President Eisenhower raised taxes on the wealthiest citizens. His administration improved the economic well-being of all of our citizens as well as the infrastructure of the country. Eisenhower moved the U.S. governmental policies in the direction of progressivism and away from Capitalism.

In order to try to cool down the Cold War, on July 21, 1955 Eisenhower proposed to the United Nations that an open skies policy be adopted by the United

States and Russia. This plan was never implemented.

Ike recognized the danger of communism, particularly after it had been successful in its conquest of Indochina. On April 7, 1954, Ike described the fight against communism as a row of dominoes. The Communist stronghold of Russia had successfully knocked over the first dominoes. A succession of countries would follow one by one and commit to communistic doctrines.

Senator Joseph McCarthy, Republican from Wisconsin, vigorously pursued communists in the government in a manner which many described as a witch hunt. During 1952 and through August of 1954, McCarthy made a large number of allegations against government employees who he claimed to be communist sympathizers. Many innocent employee's careers were either ended or damaged by his unfounded accusations. This McCarthy barrage against communism in the government finally culminated in the McCarthy/Army hearings. It was finally corralled on August 31, 1954. McCarthy had targeted the Army as a source of many communist sympathizers. The Army appointed Mr. Joseph Welch to oppose McCarthy's allegations against communist activities in the Army. McCarthy's unsupported allegations against Communists in government was permanently damaged by the Army's attorney, Mr. Welch. "I think I never gauged your cruelty," Welch declared. He went on to say "Have you no sense of decency, sir, at long last? Have you no sense of decency?"

In response to Mr. Welch's comment, the whole caucus room applauded. From this point forward Sen. Joseph McCarthy's unfounded fight against communists within the U.S. government became irrelevant. On December 2, 1954 the Senate condemned the activities of Sen. McCarthy by a large margin.

Ike was more concerned about communist infiltration into the Latin American countries. On March 1, 1954, he attempted to obtain a pledge by all Latin American countries that they would fight along with the United States against communism. He was unsuccessful in obtaining this pledge, particularly from Venezuela and Cuba. Both of these countries had already lost the battle against communism.

In a move that later turned out to be a mistake, Ike started promising more help for South Vietnam in its battle with North Vietnam. This happened on October 23, 1954. His reasoning was that this confrontation represented just one more domino in the communist conquest strategy.

On July 12, 1954, Ike's administration proposed a massive plan to provide a complete Interstate Highway System for the United States. The system would be toll free. The program was to cost $5 billion a year for 10 years. This was the largest infrastructure and investment ever made in the United States. Eisenhower originally saw the benefits of the German autobahn roadways during his conquest of Germany. The number of automobiles owned by American families after the war had increased by more than 70%.

The new highway program was to be directed by Vice President Nixon. The plan was to connect all the major cities in the United States and also provide farmers with needed farm to market roadways. Besides the obvious need for connecting highways,

Ike advised that the highway itself was needed for national defense purposes. As a matter of fact, the highways would be constructed with sections that were level, straight, and satisfactory for emergency aircraft landings or temporary military air bases. General Lucius Clay was appointed to develop a plan to finance this huge public works program. One might note that the highest income tax bracket in American history was raised to 92% for those who fell within the wealthiest group. The Interstate Highway System has paid for itself many times over since its completion in commerce and tourism. It should also be noted that there were no toll roads included in this national initiative.

On August 12, 1955, Ike signed the new minimum wage act into law, increasing the minimum an employer could pay an employee from $.75 an hour to one dollar an hour.

The mainland Chinese were threatening to invade Formosa. President Eisenhower was authorized by Congress on January 28, 1955 to take whatever military actions were required to assist Generalissimo Chiang Kai-shek and his Nationalist army against the Chinese.

On September 26, 1955, Ike suffered a mild heart attack. This unfortunate event caused the stock market to fall sharply.

In the 1956 election the Democrats campaigned against Eisenhower, maintaining that he was 66 years old and too old to run for president. Ike won the election by a high percentage of the voters and retained Richard Nixon as his Vice President.

During 1956, the Egyptians forcibly took over control of the Suez Canal from the British and French, who had built the canal originally. The British and French threatened Egypt with a military force and took their case to the United Nations. In a rare combination of allies, the United States aligned itself with the Soviet Union to prevent French and British military from going to war against Egypt.

In early January of 1957, Ike went to Congress and asked the legislators to give him power to use force to oppose any communistic aggression against countries in the Middle East. Congress agreed and gave Ike permission to spend up to $400 million over the next two years on this military initiative.

Late in 1957, the Russians launched their first Earth orbit satellites, Sputnik I and Sputnik II, leaving the United States behind in this important technology race.

With the Civil Rights Act now passed, the integration of southern schools was underway. On September 5, 1957, Arkansas Governor Orval Faubus posted National Guardsmen at the entrance of Little Rock Central High School to prevent integration of the school. On September 25, 1957, Ike sent 1,000 paratroopers to escort the black students to their classrooms. Eisenhower commented, "Mob rule cannot be allowed to override the decisions of our courts."

During May of 1958, Vice President Nixon made a 'good will tour' to countries in South America. He received much anti-American and insulting treatment in Peru and Venezuela. In welcoming Nixon back to the United States Ike commented, "The occurrence of those incidents in no way impaired the friendship between the United States and any other single one of our sister republics to the south."

On July 29, 1958, Congress created the National Aeronautics and Space Agency (NASA). NASA was instructed to start a manned spacecraft program immediately.

In July of 1958, the neighboring country of Iraq was threatening Lebanon. Ike sent 5,000 Marines to Lebanon to support the Lebanese government. He blamed Egypt and Saudi Arabia for the troubles in Lebanon.

On October 1, 1958, the United States committed to protecting the islands of Quemoy and Matsu which were under the control of the Chinese Nationalist in Taiwan. The Chinese Communists had been shelling these two islands which were close to the Chinese mainland. Ike was successful in his effort to stop the Chinese shelling of these islands.

On November 28, 1958, NASA reported the first successful launch of an Intercontinental Ballistic Missile. The Atlas rocket had a capability of delivering a nuclear weapon 5,500 miles from the launch site.

The space race between the United States and Russia indicated that the Russian education system was superior to the education system in the United States. With Ike's support, the Congress passed the National Defense Education Act. This act provided $1 billion in the form of student loans for students to attend college including graduate school education.

By April of 1959, the Cuban Revolutionary Guard under the leadership of Fidel Castro, had successfully overthrown the Cuban dictator Batista. In response to an invitation from the American Society of Newspaper Editors, Castro was invited to visit the United States. Castro's mission was to convince the American public that communistic Cuba was not a threat to the United States.

On August 21, 1959, Alaska became the 49th state.

On September 27, 1959, Khrushchev visited the United States. He made a 12-day tour of the country including Hollywood and Disneyland. Khrushchev suggested that both countries use the American word 'okay' more often during the many disputes between the two countries.

Lee Harvey Oswald visited the U.S. Embassy in Moscow on October 31, 1959. He announced that he was renouncing his American citizenship so that he could live in the Soviet Union. Oswald had been a U.S. Marine.

Many labor unions were dissatisfied with wages, work conditions, and health care provisions. A record steel strike of 116 days was finally ended on November 7, 1959. The Taft-Hartley Act limited labor strikes to 80 days. 500,000 workers returned to work. Eisenhower stressed that it was their obligation to end their labor disputes without disruptive strikes.

In 1960, the population of the United States had grown almost to 180 million people. Ike was one of the first presidents to deal with the generation gap between the depression and post-war generations. Americans who had suffered through the depression saw a nation that had been flat on its economic back transformed into the leading economic and military power in the world.

Baby Boomers were growing up in a completely different kind of world than their parents experienced. Parents were eager to give their children the luxuries and opportunities that were difficult to obtain in their own youth. Many of us who grew up during the Great Depression were unable to teach our children the value of thriftiness which had been a necessity when we were growing up.

Ike was very concerned about relations between the United States and the Latin American countries after VP Nixon's 1958 turbulent visit. Ike visited Latin America in March of 1960. He was well received by these countries. He assured the Latin American countries that the United States supported their Central and South American neighbors.

During the 1960s, many refugees fled Cuba and settled in Florida. A large contingency of Cubans had been supportive of Batista. The CIA monitored the situation closely and became convinced that a well-planned invasion of Cuba would succeed. It would include many of those who fled Cuba after Castro had gained leadership in Cuba. Planning began for an invasion of the island of Cuba. This planned invasion actually took place early in President Kennedy's administration.

A four nation summit between the Soviet Union, the United States, France, and Great Britain was planned for May 17, 1960. However this summit never took place because on May 1, 1960, an American U-2 spy plane piloted by Gary Powers had been shot down over Russia at an altitude of 74,000 feet.

Khrushchev demanded an apology from Ike but Ike refused.

The CIA had been spying on Russia and other nations, including Cuba. The plan was to fly at a high enough altitude to prevent ground-to-air missiles from shooting down the U-2s. The CIA objective was to determine the Russian's progress in the development of nuclear weapons and Intercontinental Ballistic Missile launch capabilities. The United States was embarrassed by the Powers incident. The country had spent 10 years developing not only the reconnaissance aircraft, but high altitude bombers such as the B-52 to spy on and attack potential nuclear enemies. As circumstances would have it, an alternative was available to the CIA for fulfilling this reconnaissance and attack mission. The solution was to have aircraft fly at very low altitude where they could not be detected by radar systems. At low altitudes the defending radars are unable to detect intruders because ground clutter prevents radar detection of such aircraft.

Eisenhower was very concerned about the relationship between Cuba and the Soviet Union. One of the CIA's U-2 aircraft was shot down over Cuba. an alternate approach had to be undertaken by the CIA. Low altitude reconnaissance aircraft flew missions which could not be detected by the Cuban defending radar systems. Due to the curvature of the earth, aircraft could safely fly and record important military information about Russian armaments being provided to Cuba. Evidence of the delivery of ballistic missiles and launch sites for the Russian missiles in Cuba was collected from low altitude surveillance aircraft.

The Eisenhower presidency ended in January of 1961 when John F. Kennedy took the oath of office after winning a very close presidential contest with Richard Nixon.

The most important message that Ike conveyed in his farewell address was that the country must be on its guard against the immense **Military Industrial Complex** (MIC). Having been in the military service almost all of his adult life, Ike understood the problems that could arise. The country must guard against the heavy influence of the military industry, local politics associated with this industry, and the demands and ambitions of the military leaders of the country. The country must direct its human and financial resources toward more important and achievable objectives.

Unfortunately the country has forgotten this admonition. Over the last 30 years our country has invested in unnecessary wars, construction of obsolete and useless military weaponry, and other expensive military initiatives. Unnecessary military expenditures have consumed valuable resources that should have been directed toward investment in our country's infrastructure. Infrastructure investments increase the value of a country. Unnecessary military expenditures waste both manpower and financial resources. From the 1930s through 1980, our nation spent 5% of the gross national product on infrastructure. Since 1980, that average has dropped to 1% of the nation's gross national product.

Having been exposed to the politics of military

procurement, war and international relationships, he was aware of the problem of focusing the country's resources on obsolete and unneeded military initiatives. Eisenhower's biggest mistake during his term as President was allowing the country to become involved in the Vietnam conflict.

Today, some citizens look with disfavor on the Eisenhower presidential administration. Many republicans refer to Eisenhower as a RINO (Republican In Name Only). But most Americans would label General Dwight D. Eisenhower as one of our most effective presidents. As Americans drive on the Interstate Highway System, they can thank Ike for this wonderful toll free infrastructure, paid for many times over. In addition to local and continental transportation, the highway systems have attracted millions of tourists to visit the United States and its natural wonders. Ike was a man of the people. He governed with the objective of settling disputes at home and abroad with a win-win attitude. He was well respected not only by the citizens of the United States, but by most people in the world.

Ike accomplished many important initiatives during his eight years as President. As a military leader, he understood the way the military services operate. He presided over the cessation of hostilities between North and South Korea, improved our dangerous military relations with China, initiated the Interstate Highway System, raised the minimum wage, imposed the highest income tax rate on the wealthiest Americans, held the Russians in check on the Cold War front, and led the United States to the position of the strongest economic and military power in the world.

President Clinton initiated an effort during his administration to build a Dwight D. Eisenhower Memorial in Washington, DC. The planning for this memorial is still in progress.

**Mel Barney**

# IV.

# KENNEDY

## (1961-1963)

### *Stood Down Russian Threat in Cuba and Set Stage for First Moon Landing*

**John Kennedy** was President for a little less than three years. Unfortunately, he was assassinated by Lee Harvey Oswald in Dallas, Texas, on November 22, 1963. There are those who still believe that other people were involved in the assassination, including the former head of the FBI, J. Edgar Hoover. Proof of Jack Ruby's possession of a U. S. Government security clearance is included in my earlier book *FOUR WARS.*

Kennedy 'backed down' the Russians in their effort to deliver missiles that could threaten the United States from Cuba. He also started a program to put a man on the moon before the end of the 1960s decade.

He deserves a rating of **slightly right of a balanced democracy.**

On November 9, 1960, Kennedy won a very close race against Richard Nixon for the Presidency of the United States. In his inaugural address on January 20, 1961, Kennedy challenged the country to, "Ask not what your country can do for you, but what you can do for your country."

Two of Kennedy's first actions included appointing his brother Robert Kennedy as Attorney General and his brother-in-law Sargent Shriver to be head of the new organization known as the Peace Corps. He also signed the 23rd amendment which gave the right to vote in national elections to those citizens in Washington, DC.

In March, Kennedy dispatched 400 U. S. troops to South Vietnam to help the French who were losing the battle with communistic North Vietnam. In the long war that followed, this turned out to be one of the worst military blunders in our nation's history. This military action escalated and cost the country many human casualties. It also cost billions of dollars that could have been better spent on building national infrastructure. As this war escalated the Military Industrial Complex established excessive political and economic influence on the nation. This destructive influence has remained and gained more power since that time. The war did not end until President Nixon was able to sign a truce agreement during his administration.

With the downing of the U-2 piloted by Gary Powers over the Soviet Union on May 1, 1960, it became apparent that the United States could not do surveillance and perhaps attack the Soviet Union or other countries from high-altitude. The CIA found a solution by conducting their surveillance missions at low altitude. At low altitudes. defending radars were unable to detect the attacking or reconnaissance aircraft because of the curvature of the earth. The CIA had been working with Texas Instruments since May of 1961, on a system that would automatically fly the military reconnaissance and attack aircraft at a low enough altitude so that they would not be detected. By using this low altitude flight technique and infrared cameras, the CIA was able to monitor the Soviet Union's effort to build nuclear launch sites in Cuba.

In April 1961, the Bay of Pigs invasion of Cuba, planned by the CIA during the Eisenhower Administration, was carried out. It was a dismal failure and an international embarrassment to the United States.

The embarrassment of the Bay of Pigs invasion failure was overcome when the United States won the contest with the Russians in the missile crisis of October 1962.

Kennedy was eager to improve relations with all of the Latin American countries. In August of 1961, the United States was part of an Alliance for Progress in Latin America. An agreement was signed by 19 nations and included a 10-year program to provide $20 billion in long-term financing from the United States to Latin American countries.

The Soviet Union was farther along in their development of space travel. Kennedy countered by promising that the United States would put a man on the moon within the next 10 years. Alan Shepard had been the first U. S. astronaut to enter space on May 5, 1961. He was boosted 115 miles into space in a capsule atop a Redstone missile.

After the CIA had determined that it could not deliver nuclear weapons from high-altitude, delivering these weapons at low altitudes was a better solution. The delivery of the nuclear weapons at a low altitude would allow these weapons to destroy attacking aircraft. Both the Air Force and Navy developed a tactic that allowed them to deliver nuclear weapons at a low altitude. They flew at a low altitude, used precision navigation equipment and bomb release computers, pulled-up into a sharp climb and 'tossed' the nuclear weapon miles away to the target. The weapon delivery aircraft in the meantime would turn in the opposite direction and at a low altitude escape safely from the nuclear blast. This method was practiced extensively and proved to be a safe way to deliver the very destructive weapons.

Finally on February 20, 1962, the United States successfully launched Friendship 7 with astronaut John Glenn in an orbit around earth. The United States had gained at least an equal status with the Soviet Union in this space race.

During the early 60s, many groups formed to bring racial equality to all citizens in the United States. The Freedom Riders in the south, the integration movement in Alabama, the incarceration of Martin Luther King, along with the assassination of Medgar Evans prompted Kennedy to take action. He supported an equal rights bill making it illegal to treat any U. S. citizen, regardless of color or ethnic background, in a manner other than that afforded all U. S. citizens. Kennedy supported the enforcement of the 14th and 15th amendments which supported recognition of racial equality of all citizens.

Kennedy's first meeting with the Soviet Union Premier Nikita Khrushchev was on June 4, 1961. It was a courteous meeting but very little was accomplished. Khrushchev threatened to sign a peace agreement with East Germany that would allow them to participate with the Soviet Union's nuclear programs. Khrushchev's comments prompted Kennedy to set up closer relationships with those participating in the North Atlantic Treaty Organization (NATO).

One of Kennedy's first tests in the labor competition between the management of the big companies and its workers came on April 13, 1962. The big steel companies increased the price of their steel products on April 10. Kennedy accused the companies of using their vast economic powers in the pursuit of excess profits. One by one, the big steel companies returned to their original pricing structure.

In another misguided military adventure on May 17th 1962, Kennedy directed the military to send naval and ground forces to Laos to resist the communistic movements in that country. This was one more venture into the politics of a foreign nation that turned out to be a losing decision.

It should be noted that all of our presidents who entered wars overseas ignored the very ancient and accepted military strategy that simply states, "If you are not sure you can win the war, you should not start the war." This truth has been proven over and over in our country both before and after the Kennedy administration.

On October 27, 1962, U.S. Air Force Major Rudolph Anderson Jr. was shot down and killed while flying a U-2 Aircraft over Cuba. Other aircraft were also providing reconnaissance information about the Russian missiles being assembled and prepared in Cuba. These reconnaissance aircraft provided the needed proof that Russian missile sites were being constructed in Cuba.

Reconnaissance aircraft from the United States observed Soviet Union ships bringing missiles to Cuba, presumably to launch against the United States. President Kennedy warned Premier Nikita Khrushchev that the Soviet ships would be destroyed before they could deliver their nuclear weapons to Cuba. On October 28, 1962, the Soviet Union ships reversed course and returned to the Soviet Union. This firm stance by Kennedy probably averted the start of a nuclear war between the two countries. It also assured the citizens of the United States that President Kennedy was very capable of defending our country.

President Kennedy delivered a national broadcast on November 22, 1962, in which he revealed the presence of Soviet built missile bases in Cuba. These bases were under construction and had been observed by reconnaissance CIA missions over Cuba. He announced that the United States would no longer ship any offensive military equipment to the communist island nation.

On November 24, 1962, Kennedy's quarantine of any missile or weapon delivery to Cuba was put into effect.

On November 28, 1962, Soviet premier Nikkita Khrushchev informed the United States that he had ordered the dismantling of missile bases in Cuba.

In January of 1963, President Kennedy presented a bill to Congress to reduce taxes on small businesses and lower earning individuals. He thought this action would stimulate the economy. Higher taxes remained on those citizens in the highest income brackets. The act also eliminated loopholes that allowed wealthy citizens to avoid paying taxes.

One of Kennedy's important speeches was made on June 26, 1963. It was made in Berlin at the Brandenburg Gate where he declared that, "All free men, wherever they may live, are citizens of Berlin, and therefore as a free man I take pride in the words *ich bin ein Berliner.*" ('I am a Berliner.') 150,000 West Berliners attended the speech and were greatly encouraged by Kennedy's assurance.

During 1963, Kennedy was facing many very difficult problems. He had the uneasy truce with the North Koreans. The war was escalating in Vietnam. The Cold War with Russia was becoming more intense. There were corporate labor problems. The United States relationship with some Latin American countries, particularly Cuba and Venezuela, were becoming a problem. The racial integration problem was heating up. Kennedy was also concerned about the election of 1964. There was an element of the Democratic Party that would prefer to have Vice President Lyndon Johnson run as the Democratic candidate for president.

An important step toward progress in the Cold

War was made on August, 30th 1963 when a direct telephone exchange was established between the White House and the Kremlin. This meant that in an emergency the two leaders of the country could speak directly to each other without delay.

In preparation for the 1964 presidential elections, Democratic Governor John Connally invited Kennedy to visit Texas. Governor Connally and President Kennedy were well-received at a reception in Fort Worth on November 21, 1963. The next morning, President Kennedy, his wife Jackie, and Connally and his wife flew to Love Field in Dallas on Air Force One. The Kennedy motorcade proceeded to downtown Dallas. Most of the citizens of Dallas were very pleased that our President had chosen to visit our city. People were lined up three to six persons deep all along the 10-mile route. I personally was one of those citizens who waved at the Kennedy motorcade as it passed in front of my employer, Texas Instruments on Lemmon Avenue. Texas Instruments had encouraged its 3000+ employees to observe the Kennedy motorcade. Everyone was shocked when we heard the news at lunch time that our President had been shot in downtown Dallas.

The new President Lyndon Johnson was sworn in by Judge Sarah Hughes aboard Air Force One.

Lee Harvey Oswald was accused of assassinating President Kennedy. Oswald was murdered by Jack Ruby within the next few days as Oswald was being transferred to another jail.

There was and still is controversy about a conspiracy to assassinate President Kennedy. The controversy continues after 50 years. Chief Justice Earl Warren headed a special commission to investigate the assassination. On September 27, 1964, his report concluded that Oswald was the lone gunman who assassinated President Kennedy. The director of the Federal Bureau of Investigation's Dallas office has admitted that they burned some records relating to this assassination that showed Oswald had been a visitor to the FBI within several weeks prior to this assassination. The controversy is fueled by a refusal of government agencies to open the Warren files that found that Lee Harvey Oswald was the sole individual involved in the assassination.

In the book **FOUR WARS** by Mel Barney, documentation is presented that proves Jack Ruby had official U.S. government connections. The U. S. government was the only source for these security documents. This proof includes the original documents that establish that Jack Ruby flew on classified military flights conducted with equipment developed by Texas Instruments. Only persons with government 'secret security clearances' and 'need to know' credentials were allowed to fly on these flights. Jack Ruby had obtained these credentials to observe these flights. Mel Barney was the Program Manager of this secret flight demonstration program. Jack Ruby was one of the observers on one of the flight demonstrations conducted by Mel Barney.

# V.

# JOHNSON

## (1963-1969)

## *Anti-poverty and Civil Rights Leader*

## Vice President Lyndon Johnson

was a fixture in Washington for many years and one of the most influential senators in the nation. His ambition was to be President of the United States. It was unfortunate that he achieved this goal when John Kennedy was assassinated. There was very little respect or admiration between President Kennedy and Vice President Lyndon Johnson.

Johnson's relationships with FBI Director J. Edgar Hoover were very close. President Kennedy's relations with Director J Edgar Hoover were poor. President Kennedy's brother Robert Kennedy was the Attorney General. He opposed many FBI plans on national issues, including the failed

'Bay of Pigs' invasion that had been planned under Eisenhower.

Johnson was a strong supporter of the civil rights movement and the NASA 'man on the moon' program.

Lyndon Johnson deserves a rating of **slightly left of a balanced democracy.**

Johnson had been a strong Senate majority leader and was a persuasive politician. In one of his early initiatives, he asked for appropriations of $960 million to fight poverty. He also put pressure on Congress to pass the Civil Rights Act which he signed on July 3, 1964.

On January 23, 1964, the 24th amendment was passed which outlawed the poll tax. The poll tax was a tax that the voter had to pay in order to vote. This tax had been eliminated in most of the states. The amendment required that all states allow citizens to vote without paying a voting tax.

On August 7, 1964, the North Vietnamese attacked the U.S. naval vessels in the Gulf of Tonkin. Congress gave Johnson almost unlimited war powers to deal with this new threat from the North Vietnamese. The escalation of the Vietnamese War had begun.

With the November election campaigns underway, the Republicans nominated Barry Goldwater to oppose Lyndon Johnson who was running for the office. For the first time, Ronald Reagan had entered the political contest and campaigned vigorously for Goldwater. On November 3, 1964, Lyndon Johnson won the election by a large margin.

Johnson was facing many problems that required important decisions at the presidential level. In Vietnam, the rebel guerrillas attacked the U.S. Air Force at Bien Hoa. The war in Vietnam continually increased demands for military support, both in manpower and weaponry.

The civil rights effort was growing more intense with a great deal of public attention and objections.

Large protests at Berkeley and other university campuses opposed the military draft. At the same time, the FBI had found the bodies of three civil rights workers in Mississippi who were working to register black voters.

The Cold War tensions continued to build between the Soviet Union and the United States. The popular movie Dr. Strangelove exacerbated Cold War tensions with its plot about an Air Force General who drops a nuclear bomb on Moscow.

In President Johnson's State of the Union message on January 4, 1965, he introduced his plan for the 'Great Society.' In his words, "The 'Great Society' rests on abundance of liberty for all. It demands an end to the poverty and racial injustice to which we are totally committed." Johnson's intent was to send the message, even to his southern friends in Congress who were strong opponents of the civil rights movement.

The assassination of Malcolm X on February 21, 1965, was another tragedy that drove the country toward greater racial equality.

The United States took another giant step toward leadership in the space race on June 3, 1965, when astronaut Ed White exited his Gemini Space Capsule for 20 minutes. Although tethered to their space vehicle, this demonstrated that our astronauts could not only enter space but independently move away from their space vehicle.

In a move that has been cheered and jeered by the public since it happened on July 30, 1965, the first Medicare Bill was signed. Johnson hosted former President Truman who had originally tried to implement this very important bill. The bill assured that elderly citizens who had earned the right to receive Social Security, also received the right to medical insurance. The opponents of this bill were primarily American citizens who were wealthy enough to be unconcerned about medical bankruptcy as well as many in the healthcare industry.

On September 9, 1965, Johnson followed through on his promise to improve the housing situation for more unfortunate citizens of the country. He established a cabinet level position identified as the Department of Housing and Urban Development. His plan was to provide financial assistance for low income citizens to purchase homes.

In early October, Johnson signed a bill that lifted the number of immigrants who could enter the country to a new high level of 120,000. A limit of 20,000 was placed on any one country.

Early in 1966, the United States initiated a 'search and destroy' operation in the Mekong Delta region of Vietnam. Anti-war protests throughout the country opposed this act. Many of those fighting the war had been drafted into the military services and were unwilling soldiers. The anti-war movement in the United States became stronger and stronger as the years progressed.

A published story on June 29, 1966 describing the B-52 bombing of the North Vietnam capital city of Hanoi and other large North Vietnamese cities, created more anti-war sentiment throughout the country. Citizens were becoming more and more unhappy with the military initiatives that were killing our citizens and squandering billions of our tax dollars. The Military Industrial Complex had gained so much political power that it was causing the country to overspend on military initiatives, instead of investing on needed infrastructure. Far too many young men were either killed or permanently injured, with wounds they would carry for the rest of their lives. Many citizens recognize that the Vietnamese war was not only unnecessary but was also un-winnable. The country did not have the same resolve to win this war, as it had during World War II.

During 1966, in addition to the dissatisfaction with the war in Vietnam, race riots broke out in major cities such as Atlanta and Chicago. Johnson dealt with many racial problems, however, the worst riots in the country's history took place in Detroit on July 30, 1967. The world was watching the U.S. racial situation. One Stockholm newspaper wrote, "It threatens to become a revolution of the entire underclass of America."

Public attention was diverted to some extent by successes in the NASA space program. One of the highlights of this program was the docking of two spacecraft on November 15, 1966. By the end of the year, astronaut Edwin Aldrin Junior had spent 5 ½ hours 'walking in space' after his Gemini 12 spacecraft docked with an Agena-rocketed spacecraft. In the words of Neil Armstrong, it was just like, "parking your car."

The nation's program to put a man on the moon received a tragic setback on January 27, 1967. Three astronauts were burned to death during a simulated launch sequence. The Apollo craft was commanded by astronaut Gus Grissom. The launch sequence was within 10 minutes of the simulated launch. A spark in the spacecraft ignited the 100 percent oxygen interior of the Apollo. Everything in the spacecraft was consumed by the fire.

With all of the national attention that focused on the Vietnam War, the space race, the Cold War, civil rights problems, and the program to put a man on the moon, Johnson recognized that our cities were being neglected. On November 3, 1966, Johnson pushed through Congress the Demonstration Cities and Metropolitan Redevelopment Act. The purpose of this act was to improve the infrastructure in many of our cities. The act provided $1 billion to carry out the program.

In an effort to make progress toward a more peaceful Cold War situation between the Soviet Union and the United States, Johnson met with Soviet Premier Kosygin. This meeting took place on June 25, 1967. It produced no specific initiatives to reduce the tensions between the two countries.

The Vietnam War was becoming more unpopular as time passed. On October 12, 1967, a large group of protesters marched on the Pentagon. Many of the students were injured by the military guards protecting the Pentagon. On November 11, 1967, 500 labor leaders met and called for an end to the Vietnam War. As a result of the antiwar movement by the younger generation and the continual pressure from Pentagon military leaders for a more aggressive Vietnam War effort, changes were necessary. Robert McNamara resigned the office of Secretary of Defense on November 29, 1967. Anti-war sentiment within the country had grown very strong. On November 30, 1967, Senator Eugene McCarthy of Minnesota announced that he would challenge President Johnson for the Democratic nomination. He would run on a peace platform.

It was obvious to most American citizens that we were losing the war in Vietnam. Many in the broadcast media publicly commented on that reality. One of the most trusted of all our national broadcast anchormen, Walter Cronkite, announced on March 6, 1968 in a special report that he believed the war was futile and immoral. He had visited Vietnam and commented, "We have too often been disappointed by the optimism of the American leaders." We reluctantly recognized the losing situation in which we found ourselves. Vietnam was unworthy of our contributions of our young soldiers' lives and the country's financial resources.

On March 31, 1968, President Johnson announced that he would not run for reelection in the 1968 presidential election. At this time, President Johnson's approval rating relative to the Vietnam War was less than 30% favorable. The turmoil which included war with the Vietnamese, the racial integration problem, the Cold War, and the revolt by a large portion of the college student's had taken its toll on President Johnson.

Two of the main Democratic candidates for president were Robert Kennedy, President Kennedy's brother, and Senator Eugene McCarthy of Wisconsin. In another national tragedy, Robert Kennedy was assassinated in California on June 5, 1968. In the 1968 presidential election, Richard Nixon narrowly won the election over Hubert Humphrey.

# VI.
# NIXON
## (1969-1974)
## *World Peacemaker*

**Richard Nixon** did more to end the Cold War between the United States and the Soviet Union than any other president. The détente agreement between Nixon and Brezhnev gradually led to the exchange of technology between the United States and the Soviet Union. The implementation included the exchange of engineers between the two countries.

The Brezhnev/Nixon détente agreement was signed in May 1972. My local CIA contact asked me to visit Moscow in July and talk to Russian Aeronautical Officials. I agreed and visited Moscow in late August of 1972. That trip resulted in an exchange of technology visits to big U.S. Company by Russians in December 1972 and visits to Moscow in July of 1973 by the U.S. companies for the 'USSR/US Aeronautical Technology Exhibit and Symposium.'

Nixon deserves a position **slightly right of a balanced democracy.**

Richard Nixon delivered his first message to the electorate on November 5, 1968 after a narrow win over Hubert Humphrey. His intent was to bring the country together. As historians look back in history, they will note that President Nixon presided over an administration that made major accomplishments for the United States. One of his most important accomplishments was an effective program to work with Russia to end the Cold War. He also ended the Vietnam War. Racial tensions were reduced, as well as the national debt. Nixon was the first president to visit Red China. He had many other notable successes as President of the United States. They are besmirched by the Watergate incident.

A detailed review of his administration will prove that he made great progress in bringing the country together and other important national and international initiatives.

President Nixon became the leader of a country that was in turmoil over many issues. Serious national tragedies had occurred in the election year of 1968. Among these were the murders of Martin Luther King and Robert Kennedy. Many college students were demonstrating against the war in Vietnam and racial segregation. And the country was dissatisfied with the continued infighting between the Soviet Union and the United States in the Cold War.

On July 20, 1969, the United States became the first nation to land a man on the moon. Two astronauts, Neil Armstrong and Edwin Aldrin Jr., descended to the moon from an orbiting Apollo spacecraft piloted by Michael Collins. As President John Kennedy had promised, the United States would land a man on the moon before the end of the decade. Neil Armstrong planted an American Flag on the lunar surface and commented," One small step for man, one giant leap for mankind." Most of the world witnessed the event on television. It was a huge boost in the prestige of the United States and increased the confidence of our citizens in the government of our country.

In July of 1969, Nixon began his Vietnamization Plan. The intention of this plan was to remove the U.S. military presence from South Vietnam and turn the war over to the South Vietnam government. In April of 1969 some of the first battle units were returned to the United States.

One of the most violent displays of college student dissatisfaction happened on May 4, 1970. The students of Kent State University in Ohio demonstrated against the invasion of Cambodia. During this demonstration four students were killed and many others wounded. Students in some of our most prestigious universities and almost 500 other colleges across the country expressed their outrage with the war in Vietnam.

The following year brought new demonstrations by other dissatisfied citizens. Hundreds of women marched in New York City on August 26, 1970 demanding equal rights and pay for women in the work place.

The United States finally left South Vietnam to be defended by its own military forces on August 11, 1971. The long war had finally ended. Even though the United States had ceased its military activities, some of our military and government personnel did not return home until April 30, 1975. This turned out to be a very embarrassing situation for the United States as we tried to evacuate our personnel, as well as many South Korean leaders.

The 26th amendment, which gave 18-year-old citizens the right to vote, was signed into law on July 25, 1971. The ability of these younger voters to cast their ballots made a significant difference in the politics of our nation.

From the perspective of my own and earlier generations, the U.S. government did overreact during the incidents at Kent State University and the Washington 'shutdown attempt' by rebellious students. At the time, I happened to be doing a lot of traveling around the world. A book had been published entitled, The Ugly American. I had friends everywhere I traveled. I thought it was strange that the United States had been the major factor in winning WWII as well as in the rebuilding of the nations of both our allies and enemies and yet this book reflected poorly on our country. Those who did not experience the sacrifices of all the citizens in the United States during the depression and WWII have a hard time understanding why it is sometimes necessary to impose unpopular actions against rebellions such as those that occurred at Kent State and the Washington, DC, 'shutdown attempt' by students. It is interesting to note that the military draft was discontinued during the Nixon administration and 18-year-olds were given the right to vote. Nixon won his 1972 election by more than 60% of the vote. The extra margin of victory was in part provided by those 18-year-olds who had been given the right to vote.

Nixon was passionate about trying to end the many conflicts in which our nation was involved. With the reduction of hostilities in Vietnam and in Korea, he concentrated on trying to improve our relations with Russia and China. He also paid close attention to our neighbors in Latin America and made trips to some of those countries to try to improve our relationships.

Nixon was the first 'sitting' president to visit China and Soviet Russia. These visits were made in 1972.

One of the most surprising Nixon initiatives was to negotiate a peaceful solution with China on the status of mainland China's relationship with Taiwan. His visit on February 28, 1972 was a significant achievement for Nixon. The United States and China agreed to remove U.S. forces from Taiwan with an understanding that mainland China would not try to retake this island nation.

The Brezhnev/Nixon détente initiative began in the 1970s with the exchange of technology between the United States and the Soviet Union. The Soviet Union would not issue visas that permitted any U.S. citizen to visit Russia until 1975. By the 1960s the United States had demonstrated that it could develop superior weaponry. The Brezhnev/Nixon détente agreement was signed in May 1972.

Nixon then turned his attention toward Russia and the Cold War. He found that he had a willing negotiator in Soviet General Secretary Leonid Brezhnev. On June 1, 1972, Nixon and Brezhnev finalized their détente agreement. The objective of the détente program was to develop trust between Russia and the United States. The key element of the agreement was the exchange of technology through visits of engineers between the two countries.

In July 1972, my local CIA contact asked if I would be willing to make a trip to Moscow. At that time, no visas were being issued to United States citizens to visit Russia. I told him I was willing to make the visit. In August of 1972, I visited aeronautical technology leaders in Russia. As a result of my preliminary visit, nine Russian aeronautical technology personnel visited the United States in December 1972. The Russian team visited TI, IBM, Raytheon, Westinghouse, and Collins Radio. We reached an agreement to conduct a 'USSR/US Aeronautical Technology Exhibit and Symposium' in Moscow during the week of July 18-27 in 1973. More than 50 engineers from the United States visited Moscow for this event. The group was invited to bring their wives and many, including myself, did so. The wives were treated to a very special program by the Russians which included an overnight train trip to St. Petersburg.

With the exchange of engineers and technology between the two nations, the Cold War slowly subsided. In 1975, Russia started allowing tourists from the United States to visit Russian cities. New treaties slowly ended the very costly confrontation between the two countries. The real hero in resolving our Cold War competition with Russia was President Nixon.

In the presidential election in November of 1972, Nixon won the election over George McGovern by slightly more than 60%of the vote—the highest percentage then achieved by a Republican. The nation was obviously pleased with Nixon's ability to close down the wars in Korea, in Vietnam, ease our relationship with Red China and initiate a program which ultimately ended the Cold War. Even though it had been a turbulent four years with much internal strife, the nation recognized that Nixon had made outstanding progress toward peace with nations who had been our adversaries. These moves allowed the nation to reduce the national expenditures that were being distributed to the Military Industrial Complex and substantially lifted financial pressures on the nation's budget. The maximum income tax bracket under Richard Nixon of 79% was only placed on citizens making in excess of a million dollars a year. They could avoid this high income tax by reinvesting their high income dollars in U.S. industrial activities.

One of Nixon's achievements was the signing of a bill on October 20, 1972 to share federal revenues with the states. Congress was in the habit of passing legislation that required states to expend state revenues on national initiatives. This bill provided relief to the states so that unfunded programs passed by Congress were supported by some federal financial participation.

On June 20, 1972, members of the Republican Political Organization broke into the Democratic National Committee Offices in the Watergate complex in Washington, DC. This act and subsequent attempts at a cover-up ultimately resulted in Nixon's resignation as President. Nixon resigned the Presidency of the United States on August 8, 1974. His Vice President, Gerald Ford, became President.

On January 27, 1973, the Secretary of Defense

Melvin Laird called for an end to the military draft. With the war in Vietnam ending there was no longer any need to draft citizens into the military services and conscription was officially ended. Many believe that a fair and just draft system would force congressmen and senators to think twice before deciding to send the nation into war.

In November of 1973, the Organization of Petroleum Exporting Countries (OPEC), placed an embargo on the shipment of all of their petroleum products. President Nixon tried to prevent this situation from occurring again. One of the most drastic steps he took was to place a 50 mile-per-hour speed limit on all highways in the country.

On December 6, 1973, Nixon's Vice President Spiro Agnew was forced to resign when he pleaded 'no contest' to a charge of income tax evasion. Gerald Ford was sworn in as Vice President of the United States.

To summarize accomplishments and compare them with other presidential accomplishments It is difficult to find a more effective presidential leader based upon the true achievements than President Nixon's administration.

With the Nixon resignation on August 8, 1974, President Gerald R. Ford was sworn in as President the next day. Nelson Rockefeller was sworn in as Vice President on December 19, 1974. The Ford/Rockefeller Administration lasted for a period of approximately 29 months. They were replaced by Jimmy Carter after the elections of 1976.

**Mel Barney**

# VII.

# FORD

## (1974-1977)

## *What?*

## SOCIALISM    CAPITALISM

**Vice President Gerald Ford** assumed the office of President after the resignation of Richard Nixon. He pursued the same initiatives that Nixon had pursued but with some less success than Nixon had achieved.

During Gerald Ford's 29 months as President of the United States he carried out the programs initiated by Nixon. The relations with both the Soviet Union and the Chinese communist government continued to improve.

He had no major initiatives on his agenda.

Gerald Ford is rated **slightly right of a balanced democracy.**

With Nixon's resignation on August 8, 1974, President Gerald R. Ford was sworn in as president. Nelson Rockefeller was sworn in as Vice President on December 19, 1974. The Ford/Rockefeller Administration lasted for approximately 29 months and they were replaced by Jimmy Carter after the 1976 elections

On September 8, 1974, President Ford issued an unconditional pardon for former President Nixon.

President Ford continued President Nixon's détente program with the Soviet Union's Leonid Brezhnev. Nixon and Brezhnev had three summit meetings during which they discussed the details of the Strategic Arms Limitation Treaty (SALT). On November 24, 1974 Brezhnev and Ford met at Vladivostock, Russia. At this summit meeting each country agreed to limit the number of Multiple Independently Targetable Reentry Vehicles (MIRVS) that were positioned in silos in both countries.

Although most of the dissatisfaction over integration and Vietnam had subsided, integration was still causing problems in some areas of the country. Problems had shifted geographically to the northern states. Once busing of black children for racial balance started in the Boston area in the fall of 1974, problems erupted with the local citizens. It culminated in street fights between black and white residents. Ultimately on December 30, 1974, the governor of Massachusetts was forced to call out the National Guard to oversee the peaceful integration of schools in the Boston area. On March 11, 1975, the commission on civil rights took action to reduce the confrontations in Boston, Detroit, Denver, and other cities.

President Ford wanted to end the animosity that had been built up during the military draft for the Vietnamese war. On March 31, 1975, President Ford issued a clemency order for all of those young citizens who had deserted the military service or avoided the military draft.

Positive proof that the Brezhnev/Nixon détente program was working was evidenced on July 17, 1975. On that date, a U.S. Apollo 18 spacecraft docked with the Soviet Union Soyus 19 spacecraft. This was the first in a series of cooperative space activities that ultimately resulted in the international space station of today.

An important meeting in Helsinki, Finland on August 1, 1975 included 35 of the leading nations of the world. During this meeting, all of these nations agreed to accept national boundaries as they were at the end of WWII. Settlement of future disputes would be by peaceful means without outside intervention. All participants agreed to take positive action to promote personal liberties in each country.

On September 22, 1975, an attempt was made to assassinate President Ford in Sacramento. The assassination failed because the would-be assassin Lynette Fromme's 45 caliber pistol failed to operate.

New York City was threatened with bankruptcy in December of 1975. President Ford signed legislation that authorized the U.S. Treasury to loan enough money to New York City to prevent bankruptcy of the most important finance city in the world.

On July 4, 1976, the United States celebrated its 200th anniversary. The celebration of the first democracy to last for that period of time included elaborate displays, marches, fireworks, and patriotic programs.

Other than the slowdown in the economic progress, the most exciting national news was the election in November of 1976. There were two presidential debates during the campaign between Gerald Ford and Jimmy Carter. In one of these debates Ford made the comment, "There is no Soviet domination in Eastern Europe." Poland, Czechoslovakia, and Hungary were still dominated by the Soviet Union. In a close election on November 2, 1976, Carter won the election for Presidency of the United States.

President Ford had presided over a nation that was relatively unchallenged by difficult national or international problems. He essentially carried out the programs that were initiated by President Nixon.

# VIII.
# CARTER
## (1977-1981)
## *Victim of Circumstances*

▼

SOCIALISM   CAPITALISM

**Jimmy Carter** was a peanut farmer who had served two terms as a Senator and one as Governor of Georgia. He graduated from Annapolis and served as the Engineer Officer on a nuclear submarine at the outset of his career.

When Carter took office in 1977, the country had been going through much turmoil and unrest all over the world. The United States was changing and the influences of the generations prior to the Depression Generation and the Depression Generation were losing political power to the Boomer Generation.

Younger generations had no memory of the strife of the Great Depression and the struggles to win WWII. They did not realize the shared sacrifice that was required in order to build and maintain a balanced democratic nation.

The money influences in politics had become much more dangerous. Gerrymandering tactics and re-districting polarized communities and voters, making it harder to maintain a balanced democracy with a strong middle class.

President Carter deserves **a balanced democracy rating.**

The presidential election in 1976 was very close. Jimmy Carter won over incumbent President Gerald Ford on November 2, 1976.

Several situations in the country boosted Jimmy Carter to an election victory. One was a slowdown in the economics of the country. The growth rate of the United States fell from 9.2% to 4.5% during 1976. Ford made several mistakes on the campaign trail including a glaring misunderstanding of the Cold War situation. He commented that Russia no longer influenced the nations in Eastern Europe. It was well-known that Poland, Czechoslovakia, and Hungary were all still under the control of the Soviet Union communistic regime. He also proposed tax cuts for the wealthiest citizens.

The U.S. political structure was changing. President Carter was the last democrat elected by a majority of citizens who had experienced the Great Depression and WWII. The United States had enjoyed a leadership position both economically and militarily under the influence of the generation prior to and soon after WWII. The average maximum income tax rate on the highest income earners from 1930 through 1980 was 83%. After the Carter administration, the average was reduced to 33% on the highest earning Americans. This placed increasing financial pressure on middle class citizens. Those who remembered the Great Depression and WWII also understood that U.S. investment in infrastructure added value to the country. Most understood that investment in the Military Industrial Complex added no value to the nation's worth. The average amount of the United States investment in infrastructure was approximately 5% of the gross national product through the 1970s. Starting in the 1980s this average value dropped to approximately 1%. Older voters also understood that the country is strongest when the wealth of the country is shared by a large middle class. Those in the middle class could afford to buy the products that were being manufactured by the large corporations in the country.

The nation had begun to forget the programs initiated by Roosevelt, Truman, Eisenhower, Kennedy, Johnson, and Nixon. The uplifting economics of all citizens of the country by the New Deal (Roosevelt), Fair Deal (Truman), racial integration and poverty reduction (Kennedy and Johnson), infrastructure investment and limits on Military Industrial Complex (Eisenhower), and the successful 'war ending' initiatives of Nixon.

In the election of 1976, President Ford proposed a $28 million cut. This $28 billion reduction was primarily directed at corporations and the wealthiest Americans. Those who had experienced the depression and WWII helped Carter win the election.

By 1977 Japan and Germany along with several other countries that we had rebuilt after WWII, had gained a competitive position in the automobile business. Foreign competition became a challenge for both the companies and workers.

On November 1, 1977, a new minimum wage bill was passed requiring employers to pay a minimum of $2.65 per hour to their workers.

Carter was facing many new problems that required unpopular solutions. It was costing farmers more to grow their products than they were able to gain from the sale of their products. Thousands of tractors rumbled into Washington, Atlanta, Chicago, Denver, and 30 other large cities protesting farm prices.

One of President Carter's most unpopular decisions was to allow the ownership of the Panama Canal (built by the United States in 1903) to transfer to Panama in 2000. The bill included the right of the United States to counter any act by another government that would affect the neutrality of the canal.

The United Mine Workers had gone on strike and demanded that their wages be raised from $7.90 an hour to $10.20 an hour over the next three year period.

The Nuclear Non-Proliferation Act was passed on March 10, 1978. In this ongoing Cold War initiative Carter was using the trust built up by the Brezhnev/Nixon détente program.

During 1978, inflation was a growing problem. On October 24, Carter told the country that he had a plan to reduce the inflation rate by 1 to 2%. It included the deregulation of government controlled industries. Carter figured that competition was the most powerful weapon to fight this growing financial problem.

The government ethics law was passed on October 26, 1978 which required that all U.S. legislators, judges, and members of the executive branch make financial disclosures of their income.

In an event that had not happened since the 1930s, Cleveland defaulted on its debt on December

16, 1978. One of the problems cited was the low revenue received from the city's tax base.

In response to the ongoing debate over the assassination of Martin Luther King and John F. Kennedy, the House Select Committee on Assassinations was established. On December 30, 1978, the Committee asserted that, "Based upon reports from acoustical experts the committee believes that Kennedy was shot from the grassy knoll, as well as the Texas School Book Depository."

This and many other assertions are still being ignored. In my book **FOUR WARS** (Merit Books), I provide positive proof that Jack Ruby had a U.S. security clearance on September 1, 1961. While some authorities refuse to afford me the opportunity to show them the proof of my assertion, the curator of the Poage Museum at Baylor University in Waco, Texas does have my book available in his Museum.

In one of Carter's major successes, he brought Egypt and Israel together for a conference at Camp David. The Camp David Accords was a treaty between Egypt and Israel to end the hostile relations between the two nations. For this initiative, President Carter was awarded the Nobel Peace Prize on March 26, 1979.

With the Brezhnev/Nixon détente program becoming more effective all the time, the Soviet Union and the United States agreed to the Strategic Arms Limitation Treaty II on June 18, 1979. This treaty limited the number of long range missiles each country could keep in their nuclear arsenals.

Unfortunately, for Carter several things occurred

which were unsettling to the citizens of the country.

The Organization of Petroleum Exporting Countries (OPEC) raised the price of their oil to $23.50 a barrel. This was an increase of seven dollars a barrel. It created financial problems for developing countries throughout the world except those that produced their own oil in sufficient quantity to be energy independent.

Soaring inflation continued to trouble the country. Chrysler, one of the big three automobile companies, had to be bailed out financially by the U.S. government. The difference between the wealthy and poor classes of the country continued to widen. The ailing steel industry closed 10 plants.

In addition to these problems, the U.S. Embassy in Teheran was seized by terrorists on November 20, 1979.

After Russia invaded Afghanistan on January 4, 1980, Carter shut off grain sales to the Soviet Union. A windfall profit tax was levied on oil producers in the United States. Cater had to admit on April 16, 1980 that the country was indeed in a recession.

1980 was an election-year and with all of the crises and problems facing Carter, he lost the election by a landslide to Ronald Reagan on November 4, 1980.

**Mel Barney**

# IX.

# REAGAN

## (1981-1989)

### *Initiated Capitalism Period*

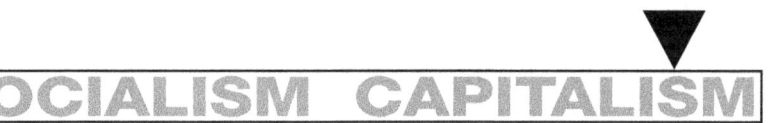

**In 1980, Ronald Reagan** faced Jimmy Carter for the Presidency of the United States.

A series of unfortunate national situations heavily influenced this election. The Soviet Union invaded Afghanistan. A windfall oil tax was levied on oil producers. In an effort to rescue U.S. Embassy personnel who had been taken hostage in Tehran the United States had suffered the humiliating loss of military personnel and equipment in Iran. With commanding influence from 'big oil,' Wall Street, and multi-national corporations, Reagan reduced the income tax rate on high earners. Under the influence of special interests, Reagan reduced many of the regulations needed to maintain a 'level playing field' for both the wealthy and the middle classes. Reagan is in an extreme right position on the Socialism versus Capitalism chart. He rated the **highest Capitalism place**.

On November 4, 1980, Ronald Reagan defeated incumbent Jimmy Carter for the Presidency of the United States. George H. W. Bush was elected Vice President.

Reagan's experience as a sportscaster and actor served him well as a politician. As President, one of his most ardent antagonists was the Speaker of the House of Representatives, Democrat Tip O'Neal. Although they had opposing views on most issues facing the nation, they were able to be friends and discuss their differences in a professional manner. Reagan gained the reputation as 'The Great Communicator.'

When Reagan took office the exchange of engineers and technology between the United States and Soviet Union was slowly reducing the tensions of the Cold War. Treaties were signed and slowly but surely the United States and Soviet Union were ending this very costly confrontation. It appeared to many citizens that President Reagan did not want to continue the peace movement initiated by the Brezhnev/Nixon détente program.

In Tehran, 52 American hostages were released on January 21, 1981. They had been hostages for 444 days. They were taken hostage by students in Iran. Unfortunately, for Jimmy Carter, this issue helped defeat Carter in the presidential election.

In one of his first actions, President Reagan announced on February 18, 1981, that he was cutting the United States spending by more than $41 billion per year. The new tax plan cut individual income tax 53.9 billion dollars for businesses and individuals. The top income tax bracket for high earning U.S. citizens was reduced from 70% to 28%. The new tax plan raised the military spending by $7.2 billion. Ultimately, the national debt of the United States tripled during the Reagan Administration.

In a reversal of the Nixon détente initiative on March 22, 1981, President Reagan's Secretary of State Alexander Haig identified the Soviet Union as the most serious threat to world peace. In a surprising move on April 24, 1981, President Reagan resumed grain sales to Russia.

After leaving a labor convention on March 30, 1981, President Reagan was seriously wounded as he left the Washington Hilton Hotel. Although he was seriously wounded, President Reagan commented to his surgeon, "I hope you are a Republican." In addition to the President, James Brady, Chief of Staff for the Reagan Administration, almost died from wounds received from the would-be assassin. Fallout from this incident ultimately, under the Clinton Administration, resulted in passage of the Brady Bill.

Reagan took a strong stance against unions on August 12, 1981, when he fired 2,000 air traffic controllers. The air traffic controllers union lost this confrontation when the government fired government personnel and replaced them with non-striking controllers and military controllers. The volume of air traffic slowed to a rate of approximately 75% of normal, costing the airlines $35 million. It is ironic that earlier in his career, Reagan had been the President of the Hollywood Screen Actors Guild. The Hollywood Screen Actors Guild was a very strong Hollywood union.

On November 18, 1981, Reagan asked for $180 billion over six years for an increase in military weapons. The measure was approved by Congress. During my entire career, I worked in products provided by Military Industrial Complex. Many of us recognized that we were building weapons that had become obsolete one or more wars ago.

In Reagan's quest to increase military spending and reduce domestic spending, on February 6, 1982 he asked for more cuts in domestic spending. His budget included a national deficit of $91.5 billion for the next fiscal year.

The increase in military spending reduced the nation's investment in infrastructure development and maintenance from 5% of the gross national product to 1% of the gross national product.

The United Auto Workers were threatened with the layoff of 55,000 United Auto Workers. On February 28, 1982, the union agreed to give up regular pay raises and cost of living increases for promises of fewer layoffs. Reagan's influence and power expressed in the firing of the air traffic controllers had fired a warning shot over the bow of the unions in the United States.

Up until November 23, 1982, television broadcast stations were limited to eight and ½ minutes of commercials during a one-hour period. Reagan instructed his Director of Federal Communications to request that the Justice Department end this broadcast restriction. The request was honored by the Justice Department. As TV viewers today know this has not been a popular move for the public.

On July 19, 1982, the poverty rate in the United

States reached 14%. The national debt was increasing at a rapid rate and domestic spending was being substantially reduced. Spending on military initiatives continued to increase. These changes in the U.S. economic situation portrayed a poor image of the world's greatest military and economic superpower to the rest of the world.

In an un-characteristic move on August 19, 1982, Reagan asked for and got from Congress a $98 billion tax hike. The hike was primarily levied on those businesses that were making very large profits. This included many in the Military Industrial Complex. Some of this money was used to reduce the increasing deficit and provide some tax relief for those citizens in the very lowest tax brackets.

Problems in Beirut, erupted from Syrian and Palestinian guerrilla fighters in August of 1982. These terrorists attempted to take over the city of Beirut. Reagan sent in the Marines and this problem was resolved by September 19, 1982. U.S. Marines were to be stationed in Beirut for no more than 30 days.

In the continuing conflict between Israel and the Palestinians, militiamen of the Christian Phalange Organization massacred between 1,200 and 1,400 Palestinian men, women, and children on September 16, 1982 in West Beirut's Sabra and Shatila refugee camps. This increased the tensions between the Palestinians and the Israelis.

By December of 1982, 18 months after Reagan took office, the national recession had deepened to the point that almost 11% of the population were without jobs. This was the worst economic situation the nation had experienced since the Great Depression. Reagan proposed a 10% tax cut and the 7% increase in military spending to stop the recession from getting any worse. The nation had reached a deficit level of more than $110 billion. These actions actually exacerbated the recession problems and continued the nation's movement toward a full-blown depression.

In a move that further increased the tension between the Soviet Union and the United States, on March 8, 1983 Reagan declared the Soviet Union as the 'Evil Empire.' President Reagan appeared to be determined to undo the accomplishments that Brezhnev/Nixon had achieved in their détente program.

Further problems became apparent with Middle East countries when the Beirut embassy was bombed on April 19, 1983. This was one more indication that the Islamic fundamentalists had declared Jihad on the United States.

A bipartisan congressional committee reported on April 26 1983 that the nation's educational system was putting the United States 'at risk.' Recommendations included raising the standards in high school and for college admission. President Reagan's approach was to keep the U.S. government out of the education system and provide tax credits for tuition for private and parochial schools and colleges. Ultimately, this resulted in reduced federal funding for the education system in the United States at all levels.

With the United States in a severe recession, our primary trading partners (Canada, England, France,

West Germany, Italy, and Japan) were feeling the effects. Our trading partners wanted to increase the interchange of goods with Soviet Russia. Reagan opposed this move, and negotiations produced no tangible results.

With the loss of the progress President Nixon achieved with his détente program, Cold War tensions between the Soviet Union and the United States escalated. On September 1, 1983, the Soviet Union shot down a Korean civilian airliner with 269 people aboard when it strayed into Soviet airspace.

In a devastating move on October 23, 1983, the terrorists in Beirut blew up the Marine barracks. More than 200 U.S. Marines and 47 French soldiers were killed in the explosion. President Reagan expressed outrage at this cowardly attack.

President Reagan visited China on April 30, 1984. His purpose was to try to improve relations with China and promote wider trade between the United States and China.

During 1984, 79 banks in the United States failed. On July 26, President Reagan approved a 4.5 billion-dollar bailout of the banking system to prevent further failures. The banking industry began a very strong lobbying effort to reduce the regulations on the banking system.

In the presidential election of 1984, Reagan defeated Walter Mondale and carried 49 of the 50 states. At that time, he was the oldest person ever elected to the Presidency of the United States.

At the U.S. Catholic Bishops' meeting on November 11, 1994, a personal letter on Catholic social teaching and the economy was drafted. In an unusual move, the Bishops accused the Reagan administration of not providing a 'just' economic system. They accused Reagan's administration of financial policies that allowed more wealthy citizens to create more wealth with the cost burden for running the country falling heavily on the shoulders of the middle and lower income groups.

Throughout 1985, the recession continued and jobs were hard to find. A growing number of citizens were unemployed and homeless. It was estimated that up to three million citizens fell into this tragic situation.

Reagan proposed a new tax structure on May 28, 1985. This structure would raise taxes to three new rates of 15, 25 and 35%. Since he had been re-elected, he felt confident that his increase of taxes on the wealthy would not create a problem for him.

As a result of Reagan's drastic income tax reductions for the wealthy from 70% to 28%, the United States was, for the first time in recent history, declared a debtor nation on September 16, 1985. The nation thrived during the 1970s under the income tax structure that had existed from the 1930s. However, with the drastic tax cut for the wealthy by the Reagan administration, this enviable financial situation deteriorated rapidly.

President Reagan met with Soviet Union General Secretary Mikhail Gorbachev in Geneva on November 21, 1985. Although they had a cordial meeting, the initial encounter between the two included a demand that the United States stop the 'Star Wars' program that was intended to protect the United States from long range missile attacks. President Reagan refused to agree. The meeting was cordial but there were no other agreements reached during this superpower summit. It became apparent that Reagan intended to reignite the Cold War with the Soviet Union.

President Reagan signed a bill on December 10, 1985, that would require that the nation end the deficit by 1991. Gradual elimination of the debt would require cuts to many government programs. If Congress did not control the budget to eliminate the debt, the budget cuts would automatically be included in the budget.

President Reagan signed into law a 169 billion dollar farm bill on December 23, 1985. This bill would provide crop insurance and long-term, low-interest loans to farmers.

On January 28, 1986, the space shuttle Challenger exploded as it reentered the earth's atmosphere over the East Texas area. Seven astronauts were killed. Being a resident of North Dallas, I was in my home when this unfortunate event took place. I heard the sound of the explosion and saw parts of the shuttle spacecraft falling to the earth.

During 1986, the petroleum companies were being financially stressed by low oil prices. The price of a barrel of oil dropped to less than $11 a barrel. Comparing that to a price of $100 a barrel today, one can imagine the risk petroleum companies faced in their quest to produce a profit for their stockholders.

On April 16, 1986, President Reagan ordered an attack on high level Libyan military leaders in retaliation for Libyan terrorist attacks, including a discotheque in West Berlin frequented by American soldiers. It was a warning to Libya that the United States would not stand by while Libyan terrorists attacked the United States and our allies anywhere in the world.

The national debt of the United States continued to increase and on June 6, 1986 it surpassed the $2 trillion level. The debt was exacerbated by Congressional representatives who were receiving campaign donations from special interest groups. The lack of transparency into the financial activities of members of Congress still exists today.

A second summit meeting between Gorbachev and Reagan was arranged in Reykjavík, Iceland. It was scheduled for October 13, 1986. The summit did not get off the ground because neither of the leaders would compromise on the United States 'Star Wars' program.

A typical example of the economic problems facing the United States was the bankruptcy of LTV, the nation's largest steel producer, as a result of the availability of less expensive steel from other countries. The number of steelworkers in the country had been reduced from 450,000 in 1979 to 200,000 in 1986.

In an action that was against United States laws and government policy, the Reagan administration admitted that it had been selling arms to Iran. President Reagan was fully aware of this illegal activity and admitted that he had approved the initiative. Iran-contra, as it is identified today, was directed by Marine Lieutenant Colonel Oliver North. A total of six government officials and military personnel were convicted of this crime.

In 1980, President Reagan appointed David Stockman, one of the most brilliant Wall Street analysts, to be a part of the Reagan team. He was the point man for supply-side economics. Nine years later, he resigned his job and wrote an article entitled "How the Reagan Revolution Failed." Some described the President has a muddle-headed leader who would rather tell anecdotes than face tough issues. Shortly after Reagan completed his two terms as President, he was diagnosed with Alzheimer's disease.

The economic situation in the United States became more precarious month by month. On October 19, 1987, the stock market tumbled 580 points, a 22% loss in value. Reagan tried to calm the nation by telling them that our underlying economy is sound.

President Reagan asked the Director of Federal Communications to eliminate the broadcast 'fairness doctrine,' which required that both sides of a controversial issue be aired on federally-controlled broadcast stations. The change would now allow special interest groups to dominate specific issues such is gun control, taxes, abortion, military spending, infrastructure investment, and other important national initiatives. This presidential decision drew a high level of criticism from both Congress and the citizens of the United States. The result was that networks such as Fox, CNN, NBC, ABC, CBS, and other networks could be highly influenced by commercial purchasers and contributions from those pushing specific agendas. It also set the the stage for the rampant bias that now allows people to listen exclusively to broadcast media that reinforce their personal prejudices and avoid balanced, professional news reports.

Finally, on December 8, 1987, Gorbachev and Reagan signed a missile reduction treaty. The Intermediate Nuclear Forces Treaty eliminated ballistic and cruise missiles with striking ranges of up to 3500 miles. Finally, Reagan was beginning to consider the objectives of the Nixon Brezhnev détente program.

The Census Bureau report on April 30, 1988, revealed a rapidly growing disparity between high-income American citizens and the rest of the population. Executive salaries and bonuses were growing rapidly while the average income of American citizens was stagnant, in some cases declining. This situation still exists today. It is the same situation that preceded the Great Depression in the 1930s.

President Reagan visited Moscow on May 31, 1988. During this visit, Reagan's attitude toward the Soviet Union and specifically Mikhail Gorbachev began changing. The editor of a popular Soviet Union publication commented, "Reagan is a simple man. He likes astrology and he was an actor." After this visit, the Prime Minister of Great Britain, Margaret Thatcher, announced that the Cold War was over. Although many would have you believe that Reagan's comment, "Mr. Gorbachev tear down this wall" ended the Cold War, if Reagan followed Nixon's lead in the Brezhnev/Nixon détente program, the Cold War would have ended at the end of the Nixon Administration, more than a decade earlier.

George Herbert Walker Bush won the 1988 presidential election and was sworn in as the 41st President on January 20, 1989.

**Mel Barney**

# X.

# G.H.W. BUSH

## (1989-1993)

## *Hamstrung by Reaganomics*

▼

SOCIALISM    CAPITALISM

**George H.W. Bush** was a true war hero and an excellent politician. During his administration, he tried to correct many of the drastic changes to U.S. policies during the Reaganomics period.

The loss in his re-election against Democrat Bill Clinton was influenced by a promise Bush made that there would be no new taxes, a promise which he had been unable to keep. The Reagan administration had tripled the debt of the nation and had heavily invested in nonproductive military expenditures. Bush's attempt to correct these destructive policies, generated enough negative bias in the Republican Party that he did not have the support needed to win re-election.

George H.W. Bush earned a position halfway between an **ideal Democracy and Capitalism**.

On November 8, 1988, WWII hero, George Herbert Walker Bush was elected President of the United States. He selected as his Vice President, Dan Quayle from Indiana. On January 20, 1989, George Bush was sworn in as the 41st President of the United States.

President Bush had declared in his election campaign that there would be no new taxes under his administration. But George H. W. Bush faced the repercussions brought on by the 'Reaganomics Revolution.' Reaganomics included drastic cuts in the top IRS tax brackets and an increase in military spending. Middle class citizens were forced to provide the revenue to offset increased expenditures in the face of lost revenue from the wealthier financial sources.

In addition, his agenda included the hard political line with Russia that had been followed by Reagan. These two policy positions, ultimately, would play a big role in his losing a bid for a second term as president.

Former President Nixon criticized Reagan and Bush for failure to support the Brezhnev/Nixon detente program. The resulting hostile relations between Russia and the United States caused unnecessary military expenditure. In 1991, the seven leading industrial nations met and invited Russia to participate. This plan was rejected by President Bush and British Prime Minister John Major.

Iraqi military forces invaded Kuwaiti oil fields. In a very well-planned military operation, Bush's military leaders retook the oil fields from Iraq in operation 'Desert Storm.'

Bush's first international decision was his reaction

to the massacre of 2,500 pro-democracy students in Beijing's Tiananmen Square. The Bush administration cut off arms sales to China. Most of the politicians in Washington wanted a much stronger response such as breaking off diplomatic relations and imposing economic sanctions on China.

Within a period of four weeks, two major catastrophic natural disasters occurred. On September 21, 1989, hurricane Hugo came ashore on the Carolinas' Coast, leaving 25 dead, hundreds injured and more than 100,000 homeless. On October 19, 1989, an earthquake hit San Francisco. The Bay Bridge collapsed, killing and injuring many people and creating a huge traffic problem for the area.

On November 10, 1989, the Berlin Wall was dismantled, demonstrating a tangible change in the policies of the Soviet Union. The Soviet Union's oppressive communistic policies were being replaced with the more democratic and capitalistic policies practiced throughout the free world. Most of the citizens of the United States realized that the Brezhnev/ Nixon détente program was the primary reason for this change. The détente program had made citizens in the Soviet Union aware of the technological progress that had been achieved in capitalistic countries.

Communistic policies in the Soviet Union were gradually incorporating competitive and capitalistic policies. Policy changes were more in line with those of the free world. During my first secret visit to Moscow in August of 1972, my Intourist Hotel room included a television set that only broadcast Soviet broadcast stations. On my third visit to Moscow in July of 1973, my wife and I were pleasantly surprised to see Ricky Nelson singing 'I Went to a Garden Party' on TV. The British Broadcast Company, as well as other international TV stations, were available.

Russian citizens were beginning to receive information about the economic and political situation in other countries of the world. After my first visit to Moscow in August of 1972, I was encouraged by the CIA to invite the Russian engineers that I had visited in Moscow to visit the United States. I arranged to have them visit my company, Texas Instruments, in December of 1972. I was also encouraged by the CIA to have them visit Collins Radio, International Business Machines, Westinghouse, and Raytheon. A typical question asked by these busy engineers was who owned all the cars in the Texas Instruments parking lot. Of course, we said it was the workers. When these engineers returned to Russia, they spread the word that there was a different and more economically thriving citizenry in the United States. The Nixon 'Open Door' strategy was beginning to work.

On December 20, 1989, 2,400 U.S. troops swept into Panama and deposed General Manuel Antonio Noriega, a dictator and drug lord. He was replaced with a democratic regime.

President Bush had to reverse his campaign promise of no new taxes on June 26, 1990 as the economic situation in the country had not improved. The budget crisis was becoming worse and Bush realized he had to increase revenues. Bush was forced to increase taxes in order to stop increasing the national debt.

Saddam Hussein's Iraqi forces invaded Kuwait

and took control of most of their oil fields on August 8, 1990. President Bush called in the forces of NATO to drive out the Iraqi forces. In January of 1991, a well-organized U.S. Army-executed operation 'Desert Storm,' was so successful that by February 28, the war was over and Kuwait had control of the invaded area occupied by Iraq. Bush wisely made the decision not to pursue the retreating Iraqui army across the Kuwait/Iraq border.

In an effort to improve the economic situation of the lower income citizens of the country, Bush signed a law that set a minimum wage of $4.25 per hour on April 1, 1991.

On May 4, 1991, President Bush suffered an irregular heart beat while he was jogging. He was taken to Bethesda Naval Medical Center where he was treated and released two days later.

Queen Elizabeth II visited the United States on May 16, 1991. She spoke to Congress, reminding them of Great Britain's participation in the Gulf War. She also visited a poor neighborhood in Washington, DC, and was physically touched by one of the children. This is a 'no-no' in royal protocol.

On July 4, 1991, President Bush signed the Antarctica Protection Pact. This was the new agreement with other nations that there would be no mining or drilling for oil or other products in Antarctica for the next 50 years.

An important indication that the Soviet Union was becoming more capitalistic happened in a meeting on July 17, 1991 between the seven most economically successful countries in the world. The Soviet Union was invited to attend this meeting for the first time. Over the objections of President Bush and British Prime Minister John Major, the Big Seven agreed to share technology know-how with the Soviet Union and the nations that were in the sphere of the Soviet Union.

On September 13, 1991, Israel was enraged when President Bush refused to guarantee a loan of $10 billion to build housing for Soviet immigrants in Israel. This happened during a period when the United States and Israel were trying to organize peace talks between Israel and the Palestinians.

Peace talks between the Palestinians and Israel were finally initiated after a meeting in Madrid, Spain, on October 30, 1991. Both the Soviet Union and the United States agreed to support this peace initiative between the two parties.

After the recession that started during the Reagan administration, financial experts claimed that the ailing economy of the United States was improving. The stock market had reached a record high of 3,168 and the inflation rate had been reduced to 2.9%.

Even though the U.S. economy appeared to be improving at the end of 1991, there were danger signs. Some of the premier companies in the country such as IBM, TWA and General Motors were reporting losses.

Former President Richard Nixon criticized the White House and the Bush Administration on March 11, 1992. Nixon's criticism was against the administrations of Ronald Reagan and George Bush because they had not followed through with his détente initiative. Nixon believed that they had dropped the ball. They were no longer trying to resolve our differences with Soviet Russia.

An important trade agreement between Canada, United States, and Mexico was signed on August 13, 1992. The three nations agreed to cooperate in their efforts to pursue international markets.

With the presidential election approaching on October 1, 1992, the billionaire Ross Perot announced that he would be a third party candidate in the upcoming presidential election. A large group of independent voters were dissatisfied with both the Democrats and Republicans. Ross Perot appeared to have the credentials these independent voters were looking for in the election of November 1992.

On November 3, 1992, Bill Clinton drew 43% of the popular vote. Incumbent President George Bush received 38% and third-party candidate Ross Perot received 19% of the votes. In addition to winning the popular vote, the Democrats maintained the majority in both the House of Representatives and the Senate.

In one of Bush's last presidential actions on December 24, 1982, he pardoned the six government and military officials who had participated in the Iran-Contra crimes.

**Mel Barney**

# XI.

# CLINTON

## (1993-2001)

## *Peace and $200 Billion Budget Surplus*

**During President Clinton's** eight years in office, he corrected many of the problems created during the 'Reaganomics Revolution.' Clinton was able to move the United States back to a more balanced democratic nation. Clinton understood the adversarial tendencies toward socialism and capitalism. He raised the maximum income tax rate on the very wealthy from 31% to 39%. He lowered tax rates for the lowest tax brackets.

He was unsuccessful in his health care bill to cover all U. S. citizens. He was able to pass a bill through Congress that would provide health care for five million children.

A 2007 Gallup Poll selected Clinton, 4th best President, he earned the rating of a **Balanced Democracy.**

William Jefferson Clinton took the oath of office as President of the United States on January 20, 1993. He promised he would follow the policies that had made the United States the most powerful economic and military power in the world from the 1930s through the 1970s.

On January 20, 1993, he announced his Family and Medical Leave Act. This act required large employers to allow employees to take unpaid leave for pregnancy or other serious medical conditions.

During Clinton's first year in office, the economic situation for middle class and poorer citizens improved substantially. In his address to the nation on February 15, 1993, he informed the public of his economic plans. He increased the maximum tax rate for the top income bracket from 31% to 39% of their income. With a more equitable distribution of the tax liability, a majority of citizens had more money to spend on necessities like food, housing, and education. This improvement increased optimism in the country and created a climate that encouraged the start-up of small businesses, new homes and educational improvements. By raising taxes only on the 1.5% wealthiest citizens, Clinton was able to reduce taxes for lower income groups and small business.

Clinton enjoyed a democratic majority in both the House of Representatives and Senate to support his economic agenda. Together, their activities created the longest period of peacetime economic expansion in American history.

The United States was already fighting terrorism around the world, and at home. On February 26,

1993, the United States was attacked by an Islamic terrorist group (Al Qaeda) headed by Osama bin Laden. Members of the terrorist group left an explosive-laden truck in the parking garage of the World Trade Center in New York City. Their intention was to collapse both 110-story buildings. Although the explosion caused substantial damage and some deaths, it did not destroy the buildings.

Note: During the presidency of George W. Bush on September 11, 2001, Osama bin Laden's terrorists flew two separate passenger airliners into the World Trade Center's Twin Towers. The damage from the aircraft collisions caused the structures of both buildings to collapse. Thousands of people in and near the buildings were killed. It also took the lives of many heroic firemen who were attempting to rescue the occupants of the buildings. This subject is discussed further in the chapter on the Bush administration since it happened on his watch.

Clinton announced his health care reform plan on September 22, 1993. The objective of this plan was to provide national health care for all citizens. A task force headed by his wife, Hillary Clinton, was set up to implement this initiative. A well-organized and well-finaced coalition of conservatives was able to defeat this health care initiative. The coalition included healthcare professionals, the healthcare insurance industry, pharmaceutical companies, and hospital organizations.

In November 1993, Clinton signed the Brady Bill. This bill required a waiting period of five days for the purchase handguns.

At the same time, Clinton expanded the Earned Income Tax Credit subsidy for low income workers.

In November 1993, Clinton initiated the 'Don't Ask, Don't Tell' directive in the U. S. Armed Services. This directive allowed gay men and women to serve in the military forces. The directive was strongly opposed by some of the top Democratic and Republican Congressman and Senators. The policy was implemented although Clinton was criticized for the manner in which he pursued this issue.

Following a close congressional victory, Clinton signed the North American Free Trade Agreement into law. This law was opposed by most Republicans and some protectionist Democrats. Clinton signed the bill on January 1, 1994.

In a move that was later mocked by opponents, Clinton appointed Al Gore to set up a website for the White House and other government facilities. Clinton issued Executive Order 13011-Federal Information Technology directive. Al Gore was criticized by many for claiming to be the person who invented the Internet. It should be noted that the Defense Department had established an equivalent but less easily used Internet system for the Defense Advanced Research Project Agency Net (DARPA NET) in 1980. DARPA-NET connected computers of major military research activities of the Defense Department with colleges, and large companies involved in military research and development. As a matter of fact, I was using DARPANET on classified programs I worked on at Texas Instruments in the early 1980s.

The Democratic party had maintained a majority

in the House of Representatives for 40 years. In the election of 1994 the Republicans gained control of the House of Representatives.

On September 21, 1996, Clinton signed into law the Defense of Marriage Act (DOMA). This law defines marriage for federal purposes as a legal union between one man and one woman. This created quite a controversy in the gay community and Clinton was accused of using this act purely for political reasons.

Clinton became the first Democratic president since Franklin Roosevelt to be elected to a second term. In the presidential election of 1996, he was reelected by a substantial margin although his party lost a few seats in both the Senate and the House of Representatives.

In his State of the Union message in January 1997, Clinton proposed a new initiative to provide health coverage for five million uninsured children. The program was called the State Children's Health Insurance Program (SCHIP). With the help of Democrat Ted Kennedy and Republican Orrin Hatch, the legislation passed. The legislation was later extended later to include adopted and foster care children.

There were many small military skirmishes from 1993 through the end of Clinton's presidency. U.S. intelligence sources knew that Osama bin Laden was responsible for attacks on American embassies in Kenya, Tanzania, and other countries. Dozens of Americans had been killed in the attacks on American embassies in Africa and the Middle East. The Clinton administration established an objective for the United States to capture Osama bin Laden. This objective was not met until 2011 during President Obama's Administration.

In 1999, Clinton authorized the U. S. Armed Forces to join our NATO forces to stop the genocide occurring in Yugoslavia's providence of Kosovo. This military mission was successfully ended on June 10, 1999.

President Clinton visited Vietnam in November of 2000. He was the first president since the end of the Vietnam War to remain popular throughout his two terms as President.

When Clinton completed his eight-year term as President, he had accomplished many things. His major achievement was the longest period of peacetime economic expansion in American history. He ended his last three years with a 69 billion dollar surplus in 1998, a 126 billion dollar budget surplus in 1999, and a 200 billion dollar surplus in 2000. Clinton finished his term in office with an approval rating of 68%. This matched the departing approval ratings of Franklin Roosevelt and Ronald Reagan. A Gallup poll conducted in 2007 named Bill Clinton as the fourth best president in U. S. history.

**Mel Barney**

# XII.
# G.W. BUSH
## (2001-2009)
### *Hubris*

**George W. Bush's** administration made five major decisions that were devastating to the United States economy and environment. These decisions included:

1. Starting an un-winnable war in Iraq;

2. Pushing through the Trouble Asset Relief Program, which made financial institutions and their executives more wealthy;

3. Lowering the tax on high income earners at the expense of the lower income earners;

4. Mishandling the Hurricane Katrina rescue and support; and,

5. Dismantling the Clean Water Act in favor of the petroleum companies and compromising the water Aquifers with 'fracking' techology.

For the above reasons, the administration of George W. Bush is rated, **far to right Capitalism position.**

George W. Bush was sworn in as President of the United States in January of 2001. He had won the election against Al Gore in November of 2000 in one of the closest races for the presidency in history. The election was ultimately settled in the courts.

Bush promised an ambitious domestic agenda that would place priorities on those things that increase the economic strength of the country. His approval rating at the start of his presidency was very high and continually diminished during his eight years in office. Ultimately his approval rating was approximately 33%.

George W. Bush was the son of George H. W. Bush. Many felt that he was unqualified to perform the duties required of the presidency. His Vice President Dick Cheney often had more influence on the policies being developed than President Bush.

When Bush decided to run for president, he asked former White House advisor and Wyoming Congressman Richard Cheney to select a candidate to run as Vice President. In what appeared to be a thorough search, Cheney selected himself. Many believe that decision was an indication that Cheney would exert more influence on presidential decisions than George W. Bush.

Cheney led the initiative to enter an un-winnable war against Iraq. According to the information presented to the public, Iraq had developed Weapons of Mass Destruction. The primary national focus should have been to track down and capture Osama bin Laden, who had admitted the planning of the attack on New York's World Trade Center and the Pentagon.

When Bush entered office, the Clinton administration had left a budget surplus of $200 billion. The Dow Jones index was 10,587. The Dow Jones average during he Bush administration was less than 8000.

Bush increased federal spending by 60% while revenues grew by only 13%. Large increases in spending included: Medicare 130%; Social Security 51%; and, defense spending 130%.

Contending that the budget surplus of the Clinton Administration was the 'people's money', he lowered the tax rate on the top bracket of taxpayers and raised the rate on the lower brackets of taxpayers. On June 7, 2001, Bush signed into law a $1.35 trillion tax cut which primarily benefitted a small group of very wealthy citizens and large companies who became known as the 1%.

On September 11, 2001, the United States experienced one of the worst disasters in the country's history. Terrorists led by the leader of Al Qaeda, Osama bin Laden, executed an attack on the World Trade Center's Twin Towers in New York City. These beautiful buildings were in the heart of lower Manhattan and housed many international corporations. The U.S. military headquarters at the Pentagon in Washington, DC, was also attacked. A third objective of destroying the White House was unsuccessful when passengers on an airliner overpowered the terrorists on board, causing the airliner to crash. The airplane crashed before it reached the intended target, the White House. The heroes on this commercial jet were identified by passengers on this ill-fated aircraft through cell phone communications with their families.

Osama bin Laden took credit for these terrorist attacks. At that time, he was located in Afghanistan. On October 24, 2001, Bush urged all nations to freeze the assets of the Taliban terrorist organization. He accused Afghanistan of harboring Osama bin Laden. On September 30, 2001, the Afghanistan government admitted that Osama bin Laden was within their borders.

On October 7, 2001, the war in Afghanistan started as the United States and Great Britain launched air attacks against military targets and Al Quaeda training camps.

In his 2002 State of the Union address, Bush referred to Iraq, Iran, and North Korea as an 'Axis of Evil.' From a diplomatic standpoint this comment detracted from efforts to improve relations with countries in the Middle East. It also created additional problems with nations with large Muslim populations or citizens of faiths other than Judo/Christian.

Many citizens believed the Bush administration was being too heavily influenced by Vice President Richard Cheney. Bush allowed Cheney to influence decisions that proved to be major mistakes, including the invasion of Iraq and Afghanistan. These invasions resulted in the slaughter of many innocent citizens in those countries as well as thousands of our own military services personnel and cost of billions of U. S. dollars. One of the most basic rules in any fight or war is, never start a confrontation that you are not sure you can win.

Richard Cheney led a propaganda campaign that Saddam Hussein, the leader of Iraq, was stockpiling

Weapons of Mass Destruction (WMD). The primary threat from these Weapons of Mass Destruction was a potential attack on Israel. Evidence was provided that Iraq was **not** stock piling Weapons of Mass Destruction. After the invasion of Iraq, no WMDs could be found. Many U. S. citizens believe that former General Colin Powell, who opposed the invasion of Iraq, 'caved' under pressure from Bush and Cheney and agreed to endorse the Iraqi invasion.

In 2003, Bush and a small coalition of our allies invaded Iraq. The purpose of this invasion was to find the Weapons of Mass Destruction. Revenue to support this invasion was not provided and added to the U.S. debt. In addition to tousands of casualties, the cost of this war was approximately one trillion dollars each year. It was however a 'bonanza' for the Military Industrial Complex.

Bush and Cheney were reelected in 2004. Bush promptly signed into law the Medicare drug benefit program. The cost of this program approached $7 trillion by 2007. There were no provisions to collect revenue to support this new national expenditure while the drug prices, coverage conditions and premiums are set entirely by the insurers.

On August 29, 2005, Hurricane Katrina came ashore on the Gulf coast., devastating resort cities in three states. The city of New Orleans received the worst of this storm. Thousands of people were left homeless and many areas of the city and its suburbs were underwater. It took four days for the National Guard to be mobilized and enter the city of New Orleans to bring needed relief to the desperate survivors. Bush had appointed obviously incompetent leaders to the Federal Emergency Management Agency (FEMA). In a gesture that was highly criticized, President Bush did not visit the devastated city of New Orleans. Instead, he flew over the coast from Texas to Florida to inspect the damage from the comfort of Air Force One.

The citizens of coastal Louisiana, Mississippi and Alabama were displeased with Bush for not observing the devastation firsthand and intervening sooner.

With the Bush popularity falling rapidly, Democrats gained control of both houses of Congress in the fall of 2006.

The Glass-Steagall Act had been repealed in 1997 under the heavy influence of former Texas Senator Phil Graham. This action precipitated the financial problems that the country faced in 2008. On October 7, 2008, the stock market dropped more than 500 points and all the major indexes fell by more than 5%. Wall Street insiders and financial institutions were making huge salaries and bonuses gambling with mortgage-backed securities and derivatives. These trades rewarded the traders with excessive commissions and led to many unwise trades. When the housing bubble burst, the underlying unsoundness of these securities and derivitatives theatened to bring down the global financial markets.

President Bush asked for $700 billion to buy toxic assets that were clogging the financial system and threatening the economy of the United States. This request came on September 20, 2008. The toxic assets in question were largely mortgaged-backed securities which had been packaged, sold, re-packaged and re-sold in the form of derivitatives, often within the same institution. What began as a practice of funding high-risk mortgages, became lethal as they were sold and re-sold multiple times. When housing prices began to fall precipitously as a result of foreclosures due to unemployment and the failing economy, the banking house of cards collapsed. Buying these toxic assets simply amounted to having the Federal Reserve Bank sell more bonds which decreased the value of the U. S. dollar. With heavy influence from the biggest banks, on October 5, 2008 Bush signed the Troubled Asset Relief Program (TARP).

The big financial institutions and banks had betrayed their investors and made huge bonuses and profits from unwise security trades. The newly passed TARP law was intended to place restraints on the big banks and financial institutions. Current policies were actually cheating the investors out of their investments. Unfortunately, the leadership appointed to execute the TARP laws were mostly drawn from the Wall Street groups who had created the problem. Although there were some remedial activities, most of the big financial institutions and banking executives kept their huge salaries and bonuses. Adding insult to injury, many continued the unwise investment practices that TARP was intended to correct. Some of these big financial institutions grew as much as 30%.

In the presidential election of November of 2008, Republican candidates Senator John McCain and Alaska Governor Sarah Palin were defeated by Senators Barack Obama and Joe Biden.

# XIII.

# OBAMA

## (2009-2013)

### *Banking Novice and Health Care Champion*

▼

**When Barack Obama** took office, the country was still in a state of financial crisis from the banking practices that created the need for the Troubled Asset Relief Program (TARP). Although he replaced some of those overseeing the program, he appointed some others who had played a role in the Wall Street fiasco. It appeared to many that he did not fully comprehend the severity of the situation and the 'iron fisted' approach it would take to correct the most abusive banking practices. One 'ray of sunshine' is the initiative being undertaken by Senator Elizabeth Warren (D) Massachusetts. Elizabeth Warren and Senator John McCain (R-Arizona) have teamed up to assist the Obama administration in correcting the banking problems.

Obama's Administration rating is **Slightly Right of the Balanced Democracy Position**.

Barack Obama was sworn in as the 44th President on January 20, 2009. His first executive orders included the removal of troops from Iraq and closing of the Guantanamo Bay Detention Camp. Congress prevented Obama from closing the Guantanamo Bay Detention Camp. Obama reversed the presidential secrecy restrictions that had been established by the Bush administration and reinstated counseling on abortion.

Obama reversed the Bush policy that restricted lawsuits relating to equal pay for women in the workplace and reauthorized the State Children's Health Insurance Program (SCHIP). This program provided health care for four million children.

When Obama took office, the world was experiencing one of the deepest recessions since the Great Depression. In an effort to improve the economic situation in the United States and around the world, signed the American Recovery and Reinvestment Act on February 17, 2009. This act provided $787 billion of economic stimulus aimed at economic recovery. The act included increased expenditures for health care and infrastructure. It also provided tax breaks for lower income groups and increased the tax rate for the top income brackets. In March, his Secretary of Treasury Timothy Geithner took further steps to buy $2 trillion in depreciated real estate assets. Obama provided loans to General Motors and Chrysler to keep the automakers out of bankruptcy.

The unemployment rate in the United States on January 1, 2009, rose to 10%. Since that time, the unemployment rate has been steadily decreasing and by October 2013, it was down to 7.3%. During this period, Obama continued to raise taxes on the highest income tax brackets and reduced them on the lower income tax brackets. This provided money for citizens to purchase more products, helping many small businesses to avoid bankruptcy.

Obama appointed two women to the Supreme Court in the summer of 2009. This brought the total number of women serving on the Supreme Court to three.

On September 30, 2009, Obama proposed new regulations on emissions from power plants, factories, and oil refineries.

On September 24, 2009, Obama became the first sitting U. S. President to preside over a meeting of the United Nations Security Council.

On October 8, 2009, he signed the Hate Crimes Prevention Act. This act demanded rigorous punishment for those who criminally-assault persons with gender orientation, and other physical conditions.

In March of 2010, Obama took a public stance that Israel should suspend its housing projects in Arab neighborhoods. This met with strong objections from the Israeli Prime Minister Benjamin Netanyahu. It was also opposed by many Jewish organizations in the United States.

On March 30, 2010, Obama signed the Health Care and Education Reconciliation Act bill. This bill allowed the federal government to give subsidies to private banks to pay off federally insured loans, increase the Pell Grant scholarship award, and make changes to the Patient Protection and Affordable Care Act. The Affordable Care Act was his signature program. It provided affordable health care insurance for all citizens of the country and was passed in both the House of Representatives and the Senate.

A minority of Republicans in the House of Representatives tried to block implementation of this bill by refusing to fund the Federal budget and shutting down much of the government. This created a worldwide financial panic in October of 2013. Many of these Republicans had been elected in the 2010 midterm elections as members of a 'splinter' group of the Republican Party, identified as the Taxed Enough Already (TEA) Party. The primary funding for this party was provided by extremely wealthy donors who were already enjoying historically low tax rates themselves and wanted to keep it that way.

Republicans have tried more than 40 times to repeal Obama's Affordable Healthcare Act.

By March of 2010, Obama had developed a more amicable relationship with Russia. With the exchange of engineers and technology between the two nations, the Cold War slowly subsided. Treaties gradually ended the costly confrontation between Russia and the United States.

In a cooperative initiative with Russian President Dmitry Medvedev, the 1991 Strategic Arms Reduction Treaty was replaced with a new treaty that futher reduced the arsenals in each country. In April 2010, we signed a new START treaty which also lowered the military threat level between Russia and the United States.

In April 2010, Obama announced that the National Aeronautical Space Agency would no longer pursue missions to the moon. He instructed this agency to concentrate on earth science projects, rockets, research, and development for an eventual manned mission to Mars.

Obama had set a goal of removing all U. S. combat troops from Iraq by the end of August 2010. On October 21, 2007, he announced that all U. S. military troops in Iraq would be home for the holidays. Hostile relations still existed between the United States and the Taliban. Osama bin Laden had not been captured, so Obama continued military activities in Afghanistan.

In July 2010, the CIA had gathered intelligence which located Osama bin Laden. The head of the CIA, Leon Panetta, prepared a carefuuly-planned operation to bomb the headquarters where Osama bin Laden was located. Obama rejected the plan in favor of one that would physically prove the death of Osama bin Laden. On May 1, 2011, the plan was carried out. Osama bin Laden was killed in the operation. DNA testing identified his body and he was buried at sea hours later. The operation also collected valuable papers and computer drives and discs from the compound. This information was valuable in tracking other terrorists in the Taliban group.

In the 2010 midterm elections, the Democratic party lost 63 seats and control of the House of Representatives. As a result of this election, the Republicans were able to block funding for government programs. Their primary target was, and continues to be, defunding the Obama Affordable Care Act.

In his 2011 State of the Union Address, Obama focused on education and innovation. His aim was to

freeze domestic spending, trim tax breaks for business and reverse the huge tax cuts on the wealthiest
Americans. He also banned congressional earmarks.
He set a goal of having one million electric vehicles on
the road by 2015.

Starting in 1997, Congress began to chip away at
Wall Street financial restrictions. By 2007, the financial institutions had abused the lack of prudent
restrictions and began to fail. The government was
forced to bail out the huge financial corporations.
Although this action did stave off a second Great
Depression, it still allowed the banks too few restrictions.

President Obama is counting on Congress to rein-
state the policies of the Glass-Steagall Act. Senator
Elizabeth Warren, Democrat, from Massachusetts,
has been joined by Arizona Republican Senator John
McCain in pursuing this initiative. They plan to in-
troduce a congressional bill that would restrict the
banking industry to those practices and procedures
set up by the Glass-Steagall Act, in 1933. This bill restricted the nation's banks to their primary business
of saving accounts and making loans. It also ensured
the savings and checking accounts of the banks' cus-
tomers. The Glass-Steagall Act protected the financial
structure of the country from the 1940s through the
1970s. It was the financial foundation for the world's
greatest economic and military superpower for more
than 65 years.

In a February 2009 poll conducted by the Harris
Interactive poll organization, Obama was rated the
most respected world leader as well as the most powerful. *Time* magazine named Obama 'Person of the

Year' in 2009 and again in 2012.

On October 9, 2009, the international Nobel committee announced that Obama had been awarded the 2009 Nobel Peace Prize.

# XIV.

# ADDENDUM

## *Authors Published Letters to* Dallas Morning News

I have shared many of my thoughts in letters to the *Dallas Morning News*, 'Letters to the editor' columns. Some of these letters that are pertinent to this book are quoted in the following paragraphs.

On March 11, 2008 I wrote this published letter in the *Dallas Morning News*, "We need interstate rail."

"I am a retired engineer who has investments that increase in value with the price of oil. As a patriotic US citizen, it is amazing to me that the only real solution to energy shortages is never mentioned—to implement an interstate rail system much like President Eisenhower's Interstate Highway System (IHS). With our oil reserves, solar energy, and wind turbine developments, we can be energy independent and clean."

On February 2, 2009, my letter published in the *Dallas Morning News*, "The gas tax should take a hike. Our relative energy efficiency as a nation is greatly encumbered by our low tax on gasoline.

Other developed nations have substantially higher gasoline taxes. A higher gasoline tax would raise revenue for rail and highway development and maintenance, reduced dependency on foreign oil, raise incentives for more efficient means of transportation, and increase the incentive to develop alternate energy sources."

February 20, 2009, *Dallas Morning News*

Trains timely in Texas

"Wouldn't it be great if we could board a high-speed train in Dallas and relax for a few hours before arriving in Houston, Austin or San Antonio? Just think of the fuel savings, the increased safety, and the lack of hassle. Our representatives are deliberating this issue now. Call your representative now to help make this come true."

Note: Those of us who have traveled all over the world understand the luxury, convenience and less expensive means of transportation that is available in most of the big cities and the developed countries of the world. These systems are valuable assets to the cities and countries for both passenger rail and freight services.

March 8, 2009, *Dallas Morning News*

Another vote for train tunnel

Re: "Dig DART tunnel under LBJ," by Joe Huber, Wednesday Letters.

"This solution to the LBJ Freeway traffic problem would do more to reduce traffic congestion on LBJ

than the "buggy Whip" idea of another toll road."
Note: One of the biggest financial fiascoes in the world is presently going on in Dallas, Texas. It is the double decking and adding of toll roads to the LBJ Freeway. This eyesore and seriously polluting project could have been replaced by modern subway system at half the price that would also have been five to 10 times more efficient in moving people and freight across the city of Dallas.

In March of 2009, the *Dallas Morning News* ran an article arguing that, "greed was the engine that drives the world's economy.'

March 11, 2009, *Dallas Morning News*

All aboard for the green route

Re, "Easy riders – Kick back and chat as the Texas Eagle rolls toward San Antonio," Sunday Travel

"This article will do more to improve the Dallas-Fort Worth and Texas traffic congestion, pollution, and economic problems than most of the initiatives sponsored by our political leaders.

It highlights how existing railway facilities are actually competitive in many ways with other transportation options."

March 25, 2009, *Dallas Morning News*,

Greed drives economic engine

With out question it is. However, greed pushes the economic engine to an intolerable speed if it is not governed. Americans who or able to succeed and accumulate great wealth, owe it to the nation to return a commensurate portion of the wealth that they have accumulated.

It is obvious that the best method of doing this is to have a graduated income tax. However, problems with the system can arise if unscrupulous people are permitted to game the system to avoid paying their fair share of taxes. This is done by influencing Congress to pass laws favoring the wealthy, investing profits overseas for tax avoidance, and hiring attorneys to gain advantage by exploiting loopholes in the income tax system. Our income tax system is good but it needs to be improved by eliminating the tax loop holes and simplifying the system.

Churn is the American way. Companies are born, rise, fail, and die. Others come along to replace them. The countries remarkable capacity for innovation for reinvention, is tied to his exceptions of failure, and always has been. With out failure, the culture of risk fades with out risk, create pivot the weathers. If you tried to save the losers, you sabotage the world's greatest economic and military superpower.

If America loses sight of these truths, it will cease to be the world's greatest superpower. I do not have the financial ability or the political mind to directly alter policy, but what I can do is tell my story and write letters to the editor.

April 5, 2009, *Dallas Morning News*

Make Medicare mandatory

Re "Some health care realism, – If we are going to have a debate, let's get our facts straight. Says David Gratzer" and "Here are five keys in getting comprehensive health care reform this year, says Ruth Markus" Monday's Viewpoints.

"Neither Marcus nor Gratzer mentioned the real problem with our health care system. The real problem is that the health care insurance companies take a far greater amount of money out of the system than the value they contribute to the system.

The solution is to make Medicare mandatory for everyone who makes more than some amount, perhaps $25,000 per year. Those with less income would be covered automatically.

I believe doctors, hospitals, and citizens would all fare better under this type of system."

Note: It is a fact that is little known by the American public that the health insurance companies receive about 20% of all the funding that goes toward all the different healthcare costs within the country. Most engineers like myself always think of systems in terms of efficiency. An ideal system is one in which the contribution to the effectiveness of the system is commensurate with how much it is rewarded for its participation in the accomplishment of the system objective. Obviously, the insurance companies do not contribute nearly 20% of the solutions to our health problems in the country. I believe a study would reveal that their true contribution to healthcare in our country would be more like 1%.

March 20, 2011, *Dallas Morning News*
Scott Burns' solutions
"As a student of world economics for 60 years who

has done business in more than 50 countries, I believe our country is on the brink of an Egyptian type of revolt, or a "storming of the Bastille" crisis. Scott Burns discusses the drastic actions we need to take to change our government to one that supports the needs of all of our citizens.

Each of us can support these changes by voting for candidates who are not presently incumbents and candidates who have the best interests of all of the country at heart.

May 18, 2011, *Dallas Morning News*

Keep LBJ all-American

Re: "No turning back – Motorists begin 5-year sacrifice until double-deck LBJ toll roads emerge" Tuesday news story.

"I hear the drone of LBJ Freeway 24/7. I try to avoid LBJ at all times. I took a hammer to my toll tag, for not implementing a modern mass transit system for a dynamic economic center like north Texas.

But I resent most the fact that the LBJ fiasco will be built by a Spanish company."

June 19, 2011, *Dallas Morning News*

"I liked Ron Paul's answers

All of the Republican debaters (6-17-11) on CNN blew smoke, equivocated, filibustered, and avoided direct answers—except one. Ron Paul was direct and brief. His most important answer was about reigning in U. S. overseas activities.

He said we could eliminate most of our national debt if we cut unnecessary bases, soldiers, troops in un-winnable wars and most other overseas operations."

Note: I do not support many of Sen. Ron Paul's congressional objectives however on this particular subject of bringing our soldiers and military activities back to the United States and closing down many un-needed military programs and facility is a wonderful idea.

July 19, 2011, *Dallas Morning News*

"An opportunity to protest

The article on NTTA'S inability to collect toll money offers the public a way to beat the corrupt politicians. If everyone refuses to pay tolls, we will have no more toll roads."

September 4, 2011, *Dallas Morning News*

Economy tilts to rich

Re: "The great speed-up - The dirty secret of the jobless recovery is that while workers do more with less, corporate profits are soaring, say Monika Bauerlein and Clara Jeffery," last Sunday's *Dallas Morning News* Viewpoints Section Points, "What a surprise – opinions run strong on tax increase," by Steve Blow, last Sunday Metro column, and "Good works, huge pay – 100 at area not-for-profits companies earned half a million or more, review shows," last Sunday Business.

As one who remembers the Great Depression vividly, I urge everyone to read these three pieces in last Sunday's *Dallas Morning News*. The U.S. economic table is getting more and more tilted in favor of the rich ruling class. The middle class and poor in our country are economically suppressed.

Please note that under Republican President Dwight Eisenhower, the highest income tax bracket was 91 percent for the highest income group. Anyone who makes less than $250,000 per year and votes for any incumbent is shooting himself in the foot.

November 7, 2012, *Dallas Morning News*

My letter to the editor was entitled: "Study the history of the depression generation"

My depression generation beat the Great Depression, won World War II in 45 months, and won the 'Cold War.' We structured a nation that was the most powerful economic and military power the world has ever known. From the 1940s through the early 1980s we prospered like no other generation in history. Following generations should study what we did to replicate this enviable period.

Note: Opposition to any increase in the tax on gasoline has been very aggressively opposed by oil companies, the trucking companies and the Teamsters Union. It is because of this opposition that the United States gasoline is so much less expensive than that found in other developed countries. Other developed countries use their gasoline taxes to add to the construction of highways, bridges, and their maintenance. Who can present a reasonable argument against the philosophy that those who use the facilities should pay for the facilities.

November 25, 2012, *Dallas Morning News*

"Mr. Kislingbury had a very excellent and timely column. He said that President Reagan reduced taxes but the national debt almost tripled during his eight years as president." Further study will reveal that investments in wars devalue a country's worth. Investments in infrastructure increase the value of the country. During the 35 years before Reagan, the amount of gross national product invested in infrastructure averaged 5%. The average of the gross national product invested in infrastructure starting with the Reagan administration has been approximately 1%. Turning guns into plowshares works and has been proved many times to improve the nations who are smart enough to exercise these kinds of initiatives."

January 8, 2013, *Dallas Morning News*

Local reporter Mark Davis wrote an article called, "Solutions are all there, if only we could find them." Davis discusses cuts in our national expenditures but does not mention the biggest hole in our financial bucket. The Military-Industrial Complex (MIC) which includes all of the armed services, large and small military product manufacturers and the lobbying organizations that sustain this unnecessary financial drag on our country.

The investment in infrastructure adds to the true value of the country, whereas, expenditures on obsolete weapons and unnecessary wars and military exercises diminish the value of our country.

January 20, 2013, *Dallas Morning News*

"Your article wages are losing the battle, by Steven Greenhouse is so true and distressful for most of those of us who make up what is left of the depression generation. We all experienced a nation that was flat on its depressed back. We rose to the greatest economic and military power in the world, and it lasted for more than 40 years. We became the most prosperous generation of all time and in my own estimation, we are the luckiest generation of all times. I believe that this success was based upon the interest of all the citizens who elected outstanding leaders to lead the country. This depression generation experienced hard times and understood the importance of shared sacrifice in the citizenry of the country. It is so important for today's generations to look at the history of what we did to accomplish this economic and military miracle.

We elected leaders who implemented the shared sacrifice concept which led to a synergistic win-win situation for both the wealthy and middle-class. This provided the new products and new companies along with the existing companies greater opportunities and outstanding markets in which they could sell their products.

Some of the most important factors in our national structure included public education, graduated tax structure, investment in infrastructure, military service for all citizens, reasonable corporate compensation, and health care.

In 1940, 5% of our adult population had college degrees. Thanks to the G.I. Bill of Rights and other education initiatives the number increased to 20% by 1950. The new engineering and business savvy of this better educated population allowed us to produce the new products and become the economic engine which was driving world progress.

The fertile economic environment created the best business opportunities in the world, as a result of the tax structure. The tax structure took into consideration the business environment and a graduated income tax structure equitably rewarded both corporate leaders and workers. The average maximum top income tax bracket from 1940 through the early 1980s was 83%. Since that time the average top IRS tax bracket has been about 33%. The investments in national infrastructure increases the value of the nation while the spending on nonproductive military pursuits reduce the value of a country."


August 28, 2013, *Dallas Morning News*

Different when it's your child

I yearn for the days when, if our Washington leaders decided to put boots on the ground in a foreign land, they were boots filled with the children and grandchildren of all of our citizens. I believe we would have fewer wars, save more children's lives and save trillions of our dollars that are needed for national infrastructure.

Bring back the military draft.

October 21, 2013, *Dallas Morning News*

No Incumbents

I long for the days of another Ross Perot or Howard Dean to step forward. Until they do, I pledge to vote for no incumbent for national office, unless they swear to vigorously pursue term limits and laws that make them live by exactly the same rules that apply to all US citizens. This includes promises to eliminate the many perks they vote for themselves.

To save the country, voters must start their "no" vote for incumbent initiatives in their own voting area.

www.ingramcontent.com/pod-product-compliance
Lightning Source LLC
Chambersburg PA
CBHW070914290526
45795CB00001B/313